1 TIMOTHY

Making a Difference as a Disciple of Christ

LifeWay Press® • Nashville, Tennessee

Explore
the Bible ®

Let the Word dwell in you.

With *Explore the Bible* groups can expect to engage Scripture in its proper context and be better prepared to live it out in their own context. These book-by-book studies will help participants—

› grow in their love for Scripture;

› gain new knowledge about what the Bible teaches;

› develop biblical disciplines;

› internalize the Word in a way that transforms their lives.

Connect

 @ExploreTheBible

 facebook.com/explorethebible

 lifeway.com/explorethebible

 ministrygrid.com/web/explorethebible

EXPLORE THE BIBLE:
1 Timothy—Making a Difference as a Disciple of Christ

© 2019 LifeWay Press®

ISBN 978-1-5359-5883-7 • Item 005815411

Dewey decimal classification: 227.83
Subject headings: BIBLE. N.T. 1 TIMOTHY / CHRISTIAN LIFE / DOCTRINAL THEOLOGY

JOHNNY HUNT
General Editor

BRIAN DANIEL
Manager, Short-Term Discipleship

MICHAEL KELLEY
Director, Discipleship and Groups Ministry

Send questions/comments to: Content Editor, *Explore the Bible: Small-Group Study;* One LifeWay Plaza; Nashville, TN 37234.

Printed in Canada

For ordering or inquiries visit LifeWay.com; write to LifeWay Small Groups; One LifeWay Plaza; Nashville, TN 37234; or call toll free 800-458-2772.

Session 1 quotation: "18 Daniel Webster Quotes," Christian Quotes, accessed February 5, 2019, https://www.christianquotes.info/quotes-by-author/daniel-webster-quotes/#axzz5egg24i5H. *Session 2 quotation:* Charles H. Spurgeon, "The Throne of Grace," The Spurgeon Center for Biblical Preaching at Midwestern Seminary, accessed February 5, 2019, https://www.spurgeon.org/resource-library/sermons/the-throne-of-grace#flipbook/. *Session 3 quotation:* Socrates, ForbesQuotes, accessed February 5, 2019, https://www.forbes.com/quotes/8710/. *Session 4 quotation:* Jerry Bridges, *The Practice of Godliness* (Colorado Springs: NavPress, 2008), 64. *Session 5 quotation:* John D. Rockefeller Jr., as quoted in George Sweeting, *The Joys of Successful Aging* (Chicago: Moody, 2008), 109. *Session 6 quotation:* Augustine, *Saint Augustine's Confessions,* book 1 (Lafayette, IN: Sovereign Grace, 2001), 1.

CONTENTS

ABOUT THIS STUDY

Deep within the heart of every true believer is a deep desire to know God better and to live the life of a difference maker. Paul's pastoral epistles speak from seemingly every possible angle about the Christian life—who we are in Christ, how we're to live our new lives in Christ, and the qualities of effective church leaders.

As you engage in this study of 1 Timothy, you'll quickly realize that the Christian life is a life of blessing, but it comes with its share of challenges, whether it's dealing with difficult people, confronting false doctrinal teachings, or instructing other disciples. First Timothy resounds with passion for the gospel, priorities for church leadership, prescriptions against false teaching, and practical guidelines for godly living.

The **Explore the Bible** series will help you know and apply the encouraging, empowering truth of God's Word. Each session is organized in the following way.

UNDERSTAND THE CONTEXT: This page explains the original circumstances and setting of each passage and identifies the primary themes.

EXPLORE THE TEXT: This page introduces the Bible passage, providing helpful commentary and encouraging thoughtful interaction with God through His Word.

APPLY THE TEXT: This page helps you and your group members apply the truths you've explored. It's not enough to know what the Bible says. God's Word has the power to change your life.

DAILY EXPLORATION: Go deeper into God's Word, building on the group experience. Engage in these daily Bible studies, reflect on the questions, record your thoughts, and take action.

OBEY THE TEXT: These pages provide opportunities to obey the Scripture you've studied by responding to questions, memorizing verses, journaling, and praying.

LEADER GUIDE: This final section provides discussion starters and suggested questions to help someone lead a group in reviewing the daily exploration.

GENERAL EDITOR

Johnny Hunt, the longtime senior pastor of First Baptist Church in Woodstock, Georgia, and a past president of the Southern Baptist Convention, recently joined the North American Mission Board as the senior vice president of evangelism and leadership. He has written numerous books, including *Demolishing Strongholds*.

ABOUT 1 TIMOTHY

The apostle Paul became acquainted with Timothy during his second missionary journey. He referred to him as his "true son in the faith" (1 Tim. 1:2). Paul's affection and confidence in Timothy were demonstrated by the responsibilities he gave him. Timothy was assigned leadership for churches in Thessalonica (see 1 Thess. 3:2), Corinth (see Acts 18:5), and Ephesus (see Acts 19:22), although Timothy's primary area of ministry was Ephesus.

Paul most likely wrote 1 Timothy during his ministry in the region of Macedonia (see 1 Tim. 1:3) as Timothy ministered in Ephesus, probably around AD 63. This date falls between Paul's two imprisonments in Rome.

Paul had a threefold purpose in his message to Timothy:

1. Paul instructed and advised him to refute the false teaching that threatened the health and mission of the church in Ephesus.

2. Paul encouraged him to select godly leaders to minister effectively to the congregation.

3. Paul purposefully emphasized the union of belief and behavior. Sound doctrine is to be accentuated by a Christlike lifestyle.

For helps on how to use *Explore the Bible,* tips on how to better lead groups, or additional ideas for leading, visit ministrygrid.com/web/explorethebible.

Entrusted

As recipients of God's grace, believers are entrusted with the truth of the gospel message.

1 Timothy 1:3-17

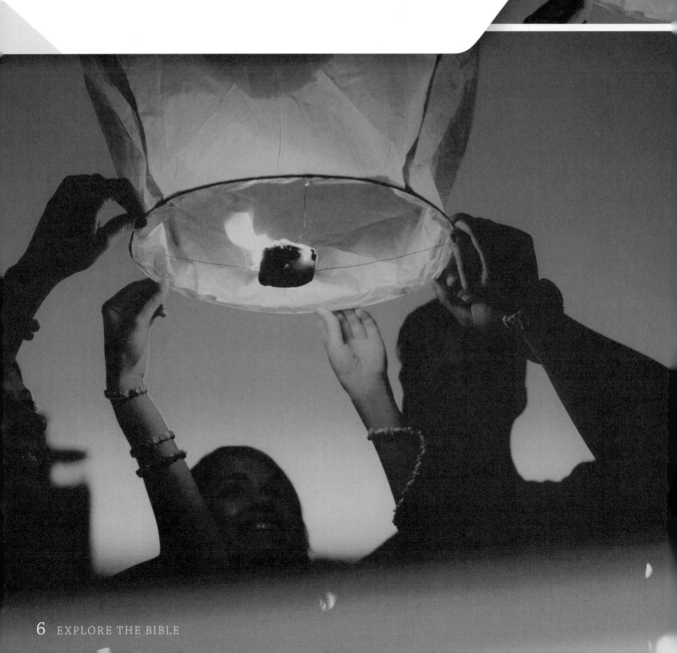

What family recipes, stories, or traditions have been entrusted to you? How does your knowing those items foster a sense of responsibility to other family members?

Daniel Webster is regarded as an epic statesmen in American history. On one occasion he was asked about the most profound thought that had ever occupied his mind. Webster solemnly replied, "My personal responsibility to God." As followers of Christ, we feel a solemn responsibility to honor His truth. We've been entrusted with the priceless treasure of the gospel. He has given us the sacred privilege of guarding, living, and sharing His truth.

❯ UNDERSTAND THE CONTEXT

Paul met Timothy on a second missionary journey as he traveled through Lystra (see Acts 16:1-3). Timothy was highly esteemed among the followers of Christ in the area around Lystra and Derbe. Consequently, Paul invited him to join his missionary team as they spread the gospel throughout the Roman Empire. Several years later Paul trusted Timothy with the pastoral work in Ephesus and with confronting false teachers who threatened the church.

Ephesus was one of the foremost cities in the Roman Empire, ranking in status just below Rome and Athens. The city was known for its idolatrous worship in the temple of Artemis (also called the temple of Diana). The worship of Diana provided a lucrative business among silversmiths, who crafted idols and other objects of worship. The Roman deity Diana, the counterpart of the Greek goddess Artemis, was a nature and fertility deity invoked for hunting and pregnancy. During Paul's lengthy ministry in Ephesus, a leader among the silversmiths named Demetrius organized a resistance movement against Paul's preaching (see Acts 19:21-41). Demetrius rightly argued that Paul preached against idolatry and objects crafted by hand to serve as gods. The silversmiths' real fear, however, was financial and nationalistic. If people believed the gospel Paul preached, they would cease their practice of idolatry. If the practice of idolatry stopped, then profit sales would plunge, and Diana would no longer be the main attraction for devotees throughout Asia Minor. Consequently, a riot occurred, and the city was filled confusion while the people shouted, "Great is Artemis of the Ephesians!" for two hours (see Acts 19:28,34).

Timothy needed to be strong and courageous in this cosmopolitan culture steeped in pagan idolatry and sexual immorality. Paul charged him with the task of refuting teachers in Ephesus who spread doctrines contrary to the true gospel.

› 1 TIMOTHY 1:3-17

3 As I urged you when I went to Macedonia, remain in Ephesus so that you may instruct certain people not to teach false doctrine **4** or to pay attention to myths and endless genealogies. These promote empty speculations rather than God's plan, which operates by faith. **5** Now the goal of our instruction is **love Ⓐ** that comes from a pure heart, a good conscience, and a sincere faith. **6** Some have departed from these and turned aside to fruitless discussion. **7** They want to be **teachers of the law Ⓑ**, although they don't understand what they are saying or what they are insisting on. **8** But we know that the law is good, provided one uses it legitimately. **9** We know that the law is not meant for **a righteous person Ⓒ**, but for the lawless and rebellious, for the ungodly and sinful, for the unholy and irreverent, for those who kill their fathers and mothers, for murderers, **10** for the sexually immoral and homosexuals, for slave traders, liars, perjurers, and for whatever else is contrary to the sound teaching **11** that conforms to the **gospel Ⓓ** concerning the glory of the blessed God, which was entrusted to me. **12** I give thanks to Christ Jesus our Lord who has strengthened me, because he considered me faithful, appointing me to the ministry— **13** even though I was formerly a blasphemer, a persecutor, and an arrogant man. But I received mercy because I acted out of ignorance in unbelief, **14** and the **grace Ⓔ** of our Lord overflowed, along with the faith and love that are in Christ Jesus. **15** This saying is trustworthy and deserving of full acceptance: "Christ Jesus came into the world to save sinners"—and I am the worst of them. **16** But I received mercy for this reason, so that in me, the worst of them, Christ Jesus might demonstrate his extraordinary patience as an example to those who would believe in him for eternal life. **17** Now to the King eternal, immortal, invisible, the only God, be honor and glory forever and ever. Amen.

Passage Outline

Accountable
(1 Tim. 1:3-7)

In Light of the Gospel
(1 Tim. 1:8-11)

In Response to His Grace
(1 Tim. 1:12-17)

Keywords

Ⓐ From devoting themselves to God's Word, they would grow stronger in God's love for them, prompting them to love Him and one another (see Matt. 22:36-40).

Ⓑ Experts who instructed people in the law of Moses. Like the Pharisees, teachers of the law confronted Jesus in His ministry.

Ⓒ All people who've been made right with God through Jesus Christ. When they repented and placed their faith in Christ, He made them righteous.

Ⓓ God's gift of salvation through Christ alone must remain the bedrock of their faith and instruction.

Ⓔ Instead of being rightly punished, Paul received what he never deserved— new life in Christ.

❯ EXPLORE THE TEXT

Paul entrusted to Timothy the task of faithfully teaching the gospel message in a church that was susceptible to deception and doctrinal heresy. Serious perversions of the gospel threatened not only the health of the church but also the message of salvation. Paul reminded Timothy of the aim of gospel teaching. That goal is love. Unlike the crafty false teachers who were motivated by selfishness, Paul emphasized the necessity of sacrificial love. He chose the Greek word *agape* to express self-denying devotion to God that overflows to others. The false teachers had strayed from genuine love. The inevitable result was fruitless discussion. Their teaching omitted the essential content of the gospel and led to unproductive conversations.

What responsibility do teachers have to the people they teach? What responsibility does the person being taught have to the person teaching?

Paul explained that the law is good when used legitimately. God's law operated like a bright light that exposed the filth hidden by darkness. Paul illustrated this point by citing a list of sins prohibited in the Ten Commandments.

How does the law point to our need for a Savior? How does Jesus provide what the law couldn't provide?

Paul was deeply thankful that Jesus strengthened him. The Lord's strength enabled Paul to share the gospel despite hardships and sustained him during times of suffering. Timothy must have been keenly aware that Paul's message was written from the squalor of a Roman prison as a testimony to the Lord's enduring grace. Paul also gratefully rejoiced that the Lord had given him the privilege to serve in the mission of proclaiming the gospel. Paul believed he was a steward. He never considered ministry to be a title he earned. It was a gift to be stewarded and utilized as the Lord intended.

How does a person's past serve as a means for God to demonstrate His mercy and grace? How does a person's past become a source of gratitude for salvation?

Paul stated that his salvation was meant to serve as an example of the extravagant patience of Christ to all others who might believe in Him for eternal life. Essentially, Paul's point was this: if Jesus would and could save someone like him, given who he had been and what he had done, Jesus is able to save anyone.

How did Paul's life become an exhibit of God's grace and mercy?

> **BIBLE SKILL: Read a related passage to gain insight.** >> Read Romans 5:20–6:4; 7:14-25. Put yourself in Paul's shoes as you consider your own life. What's your emotional reaction to an awareness of sin? How does it produce humility and a deep sense of need for God's grace? How does it cause you to be more humble toward other people? Record a prayer expressing your gratitude and commitment to the Lord for His grace.

❯ APPLY THE TEXT

> ❯ Teachers are accountable to the church and to God.

> ❯ Salvation is found only through faith in Jesus.

> ❯ Believers exhibit God's grace and mercy for all people to see.

Discuss with your group ways of holding one another accountable for remaining focused on the gospel. Identify actions the group can take to guard against being distracted by controversies and pointless debates.

Reflect on 1 Timothy 1:15. Quote the verse while looking at a photo of yourself. Record your emotions. Memorize the verse.

Identify one person with whom you can share the gospel. What steps will you take to share with the person you identified. Assign dates to your steps.

❯ DAILY EXPLORATION

Day 1: Beware of false teachers.

Read 1 Timothy 1:3-4, noting Paul's instructions to Timothy.

Years earlier Paul had warned the Ephesian church leaders that false teachers would rise up within the church and lure believers away by deviant doctrines (see Acts 20:29-30). The tragic result of deviant doctrines is the promotion of empty speculation. Irrelevant, trivial conjecture sidelines the teaching of the gospel. This truth flashes like a caution signal for the church today. It warns us to avoid two equal and opposite pitfalls:

1. The temptation of enticing doctrine unsubstantiated by God's Word

2. The seductive lure of pointless speculation that consumes our time and energy at the expense of sharing the gospel

What responsibility does a teacher have to you as a learner?

Day 2: The aim of the gospel is love.

Read 1 Timothy 1:5-7, highlighting the word love.

Paul reminded Timothy that the aim of gospel teaching is love. Paul cited three qualities of this love.

1. It flows from "a pure heart" (v. 5). Jesus purifies believers at conversion. However, believers are also empowered to embrace purity as they grow in grace daily. Love from a pure heart enhances right relationships.

2. It produces "a good conscience" (v. 5). A conscience clouded by pride and prejudice impairs love, but a clean conscience edifies other people and strengthens relationships.

3. It produces "a sincere faith" (v. 5). The adjective *sincere* points to a faith free from hypocrisy.

The false teachers had strayed from genuine love. The inevitable result was fruitless discussion. Their teaching omitted the essential content of the gospel and led to unproductive conversations. These false teachers aspired to be teachers of the law but were clueless about the meaning and purpose of the law. They steered listeners away from the truth of God's Word. Moreover, they missed the objective of the Old Testament: to point to Jesus as the Messiah. Teachers and preachers should allow nothing to obscure the faithful interpretation and communication of God's saving work through Christ.

Why is it important to recognize and confront people who teach a different doctrine?

Day 3: Jesus fulfilled the law in our place.

Read 1 Timothy 1:8-11, considering what Paul said the law is and is not.

Paul explained that the law is good when used legitimately.

1. The law reflects God's will. God gave it to show how He wants His people to live.

2. The law serves as God's plumb line. It was designed to reveal whether we're correctly aligned with Him. However, just as a plumb line can't make a crooked wall straight, the law can't make us straight before God.

3. The law points to the Savior who perfectly fulfilled it without sin.

Paul said the gospel had been entrusted to him. Unlike the self-appointed teachers who spread a false message, Paul courageously stood on the truth of the gospel. Not only was the gospel entrusted to Paul, but it's also entrusted to every follower of Christ.

> **KEY DOCTRINE: Man** >> Through the temptation of Satan, man transgressed God's command and fell from his original innocence, whereby his posterity inherits a nature and an environment inclined toward sin (see 1 Cor. 15:21-22).

How does the law point to your need for a Savior? How does Jesus provide what the law couldn't provide?

Day 4: God can use your past for His glory.

Read 1 Timothy 1:12-14, noticing Paul's history.

Every salvation story is written against the stained backdrop of sin. Paul didn't flinch to tell his story of having once been "a blasphemer, a persecutor, and an arrogant man" (v. 13). As a blasphemer, Paul had rejected Jesus and had persuaded others to do the same. He was a persecutor who had tried to destroy Christians (see Acts 8:3) and had persecuted them to their deaths (see Acts 22:4). Furthermore, he had personified arrogance and insolence. He had behaved like a bully, taunting frightened believers.

Paul was delivered from his ignorance and unbelief because God showed him mercy. He was a highly intellectual, devoted Pharisee, but he was ignorant of the true identity of Jesus. His ignorance wasn't an excuse to justify his past but evidence of his need for God's mercy. Mercy and grace are twin attributes of God's character, but they provide slightly different effects. Grace is God's giving us what we don't deserve: salvation and eternity with Him. Mercy is God's withholding from us what we deserve: His wrath and eternity without Him. Paul testified that the Lord's grace overflowed in his life. It was like a gushing river of love that surged by faith into his dry, parched soul.

How does your past serve as a means for God to demonstrate His mercy and grace? How does your past become a source of gratitude for your salvation?

Day 5: Jesus came to save sinners.

Read 1 Timothy 1:15-17, identifying what Paul said is trustworthy.

The only places in the New Testament where Paul used the phrase "This saying is trustworthy" (v. 15) are in his epistles to Timothy and Titus. This trustworthy statement, which declares a nonnegotiable truth to be embraced, reveals the reason Jesus came to earth: to save sinners. His ultimate, primary mission was salvation. As Paul continued reflecting on the saving grace of God in Christ, his writing erupted in praise. He stacked attribute on attribute, calling God "the King eternal" (v. 17), a term that described God as the supreme Ruler for all time. He also referred to God as immortal because He never deteriorates or decays when everything else fades into obscurity. Paul characterized God as invisible and as "the only God" (v. 17). God is Spirit, but He revealed Himself in Jesus, and He has no competitor or rival. Paul responded to this truth by declaring God alone to be worthy of all honor and glory.

How does your life exhibit God's grace and mercy?

> *The most important thought that ever occupied my mind is that of my individual responsibility to God.*
>
> DANIEL WEBSTER

❯ OBEY THE TEXT

Reflect on the truths found in 1 Timothy 1 and record your responses to the following questions or discuss them with two other members of your Bible-study group.

In what ways are the threats to the gospel message that Paul identified to Timothy still risks today?

In what ways have you seen the law used for good?

Why is a personal testimony such a rich, powerful tool for communicating the truths of the gospel?

MEMORIZE

This saying is trustworthy and deserving of full acceptance: "Christ Jesus came into the world to save sinners"—and I am the worst of them.

1 TIMOTHY 1:15

MY THOUGHTS

Record insights and questions from this session's group experience and daily exploration.

_____

_____

_____

_____

_____

_____

_____

MY RESPONSE

Note specific ways you'll put into practice the truth explored this week.

_____

_____

_____

_____

_____

_____

_____

MY PRAYERS

List specific prayer needs and answers to remember this week.

_____

_____

_____

_____

_____

_____

_____

On Mission

Believers are to be mindful of how they represent God in the world.

1 Timothy 2

When have you become aware that someone was watching you? How did that awareness change your behavior?

Everywhere we go, someone is watching us. A family member, a child, a friend, a coworker—someone is watching. This watching isn't being done in a weird way, but it's done to see how we do things, especially if we claim to be Christians. Not only are our actions being watched, but so are our attitudes and motives. People want to know whether our Christian lives are genuine, so they watch us. Jesus gives us opportunities to influence others for Him by representing Him in this world.

❯ UNDERSTAND THE CONTEXT

Sandwiched between his warning about resisting false teachers (see 1 Tim. 1) and his instructions about qualifications for pastors and deacons (see 1 Tim. 3), Paul urged Timothy to lead the Ephesian believers to develop lifestyles that would influence their community for Christ. From prayer and worship to the way they dressed and behaved, Ephesian believers had opportunities for witnessing to people caught up in the pagan culture of their city.

Setting a godly example as representatives of Christ would be essential for both men and women in the church. Paul expected men to practice godliness. Effective prayer is connected to the pursuit of holiness. Likewise, women were challenged to pursue godliness by the way they presented themselves to others. The temple of Diana threw a licentious shadow over the culture of Ephesus. Prostitutes dressed provocatively to lure men into immorality. Paul didn't want the female followers of Christ to imitate such scandalous attire. Modesty is the style of dress for women who represent Christ.

Furthermore, Paul gave guidelines about male and female roles. Both men and women are to practice submission to Christ. Paul honored women by treating them as equally capable of learning as men. However, given the Ephesian culture and his missionary mindset, he instructed them to exercise restraint by demonstrating a quiet demeanor. A boisterous, contentious disposition, such as some false teachers advocated, wasn't an appropriate testimony for a woman who was fully surrendered to Christ. Moreover, Paul didn't want women to exert a domineering, distasteful authority that would hinder the spread of the gospel.

Godly lifestyles and faithful worship would authenticate the faith the Ephesians proclaimed. By any and all means, they were on mission to Ephesus and beyond.

➤ 1 TIMOTHY 2

1 First of all, then, I urge that petitions, prayers, intercessions, and thanksgivings be made for everyone, **2** for kings and all those who are in authority, so that we may lead a tranquil and quiet life in all godliness and **dignity** Ⓐ. **3** This is good, and it pleases God our Savior, **4** who wants everyone to be saved and to come to the knowledge of the truth. **5** For there is one God and one mediator between God and humanity, the man Christ Jesus, **6** who gave himself as a ransom for all, a testimony at the proper time. **7** For this I was appointed a herald, an apostle (I am telling the truth; I am not lying), and a teacher of the Gentiles in faith and truth. **8** Therefore, I want the men in every place to pray, lifting up holy hands without anger or argument. **9** Also, the women are to dress themselves in modest clothing, with decency and good sense, not with elaborate hairstyles, gold, pearls, or expensive apparel, **10** but with **good works** Ⓑ, as is proper for women who profess to worship God. **11** A woman is to learn quietly with full **submission** Ⓒ. **12** I do not allow a woman to teach or to have authority over a man; instead, she is to remain quiet. **13** For Adam was **formed first** Ⓓ, then Eve. **14** And Adam was not deceived, but the woman was deceived and transgressed. **15** But she will be **saved through childbearing** Ⓔ, if they continue in faith, love, and holiness, with good sense.

Passage Outline

Through Prayer
(1 Tim. 2:1-7)

Led by Godly Men
(1 Tim. 2:8)

Supported by Godly Women
(1 Tim. 2:9-15)

Keywords

Ⓐ Paul wanted Christians to be respected by people in power and church leaders to behave in a manner worthy of respect (see 1 Tim. 2:1-2; 3:4,8,11).

Ⓑ Godly actions; whatever they did would call attention to or detract from God's living in them.

Ⓒ The term isn't meant to belittle women but emphasizes the need for "humility" (GNT).

Ⓓ Paul used Adam and Eve to explain his approach to orderly behavior for Christians who gather to worship and serve Him (see 1 Cor. 11:7-9).

Ⓔ Men and woman alike are saved by giving their lives to Jesus. However, a Christian woman embraces her unique role in bringing children into the world and strives to grow toward spiritual maturity.

❯ EXPLORE THE TEXT

Paul urged Timothy to make prayer a priority in his life and in the church. God is pleased when believers pray for everyone to know Him as Savior. The statement "There is one God" (1 Tim. 2:5) declares God's uniqueness. It served as a rebuke to the plurality of idols in Ephesus. God is the one and only God who has no rival. Because He's the one God, He alone can provide the way of salvation through His Son, our Savior. The extent of His salvation includes all who respond to Him by faith. None are denied reconciliation with God except those who deny their need for His forgiveness and refuse His grace provided through Christ Jesus.

How should the gospel's offer to all people affect the way we pray?

Our passion for Christ can be gauged by our commitment to His mission. Our commitment to His mission can be measured by our faithfulness in prayer. Consequently, Paul challenged men to pray with arms outstretched and without anger. A church full of men holding resentment toward one another can't advance the mission of Christ.

How can anger influence a person's prayer requests? How does anger get in the way of prayer?

Women and men are both created in the image of God and hold equal status before Him. God created them to hold different but no less important roles according to His purpose. Both men and women are to demonstrate godliness. Many pagan women in Ephesus adorned themselves seductively. By contrast, Paul wanted women who had been transformed by Christ to affirm the inward reality of their salvation by their outward appearance and faithful deeds. Modesty and self-control are appropriate guidelines for all believers.

How does clothing reveal what people feel about themselves? How can clothing choices be a positive influence for Christ? Do they really matter? Explain.

Paul took the opportunity to instruct Timothy in the way women should act in the church. Much of the unnecessary controversy surrounding these verses has centered on the word *submission* (see v. 11). Jesus modeled submission and was no less God the Son because He submitted to the Father. Moreover, women played a crucial role in Jesus' ministry. Without women fulfilling their God-assigned role, men would be hindered in their God-assigned tasks as spiritual leaders in the home and the church.

> **BIBLE SKILL: Use a concordance and Bible dictionary.** >> Using a concordance, find other passages dealing with the different roles each gender has in church life and ministry. Review an article on gender equality in a Bible dictionary. Record a description of the roles men and women have in fulfilling the church's mission. What are some similarities? What are some differences? Why is prayer so important for both men and women in fulfilling Christ's commission?

❯ APPLY THE TEXT

> ❯ Believers are to pray with a focus on the lost.

> ❯ Godly men are to set the example in praying for others.

> ❯ Godly women are to be mindful of ways their dress and actions affect the witness of the church.

As a group, discuss ways to be more intentional in praying for the salvation of others. How can your group consistently pray for the lost in your community?

Reflect on your attitude toward and motives for prayer. What changes do you need to make in order to follow the directives about prayer in this passage?

Take time to pray, asking God to reveal any of your actions that might interfere with sharing the gospel. Commit to make changes as He reveals those actions to you. Record any plans you make as a result of what God reveals to you.

❯ DAILY EXPLORATION

Day 1: Prayer should be a priority for all believers.

Read 1 Timothy 2:1-4, highlighting verse 1.

Paul urged Timothy to make prayer a priority in his life and in the church. The phrase "First of all" (v. 1) emphasized the essential role of prayer. In verse 1 the term *petitions* denoted specific requests to God about spiritual needs. The word *prayers* was a comprehensive expression for all types of appeals to God. *Intercessions* indicated an intervention on behalf of someone, while *thanksgivings* expressed profound gratitude to God for His grace and goodness. Moreover, the scope of prayer extended to everyone.

Although prayers were to be offered for everyone, kings and others in authority stood in special need because of the responsibility they carried and the influence they exercised. Paul's exhortation came at a time when Nero wielded uncontested power in Rome. As the tide of persecution rose, it was imperative to pray for governing officials. God can achieve more through our prayers for leaders than we can achieve through our own plans regarding them.

What kinds of prayers do you think the world most wants? What would God want for humankind?

Day 2: Jesus' gift of salvation is for all people.

Read 1 Timothy 2:5-7, considering the people for whom Jesus gave up His life.

Jesus died an atoning death for our sin. Jesus' death paid the price to release us from the penalty of death and sin. He offered Himself on the cross as our substitute by dying for sin on our behalf. Once again, the extent of His salvation included all who respond to Him by faith. None are denied reconciliation with God except those who deny their need for His forgiveness and refuse His grace provided through Christ Jesus.

Similarly, in verse 7 Paul affirmed his testimony of the gospel message as a man whom Christ appointed for a threefold mission.

1. Paul was a herald, someone proclaiming to everyone a crucial message about Jesus' victory.

2. Paul was an apostle, someone commissioned by the Lord and sent out with full authority to exercise a task.

3. Paul was a teacher, instructing the Gentiles in faith and truth. The inclusion of Gentiles indicated that the scope of the gospel was for everyone and wasn't limited to the Jews. Therefore, Paul reinforced the necessity of praying for all people because all people need to hear the truth about Jesus and to place their faith in Him.

How should the gospel's offer to all people affect the way you pray?

Day 3: Don't let anger impede prayers.

Read 1 Timothy 2:8, noting the specific instructions about prayer.

In view of the threats against the church from false teachers inside and antagonists outside, Paul wanted men to pray whenever and wherever believers gathered for worship. The phrase "Lifting up holy hands" referred more to purity of the heart than to the posture of the body. A man who passionately strives to honor God can effectively pray with hands folded or hands lifted. Although standing with hands outstretched toward heaven was a customary practice for prayer, Paul specified that it was to be done without anger or argument. A church full of men holding resentment toward one another can't advance the mission of Christ. Men who argue with one another rather than pray for one another stifle the spread of the gospel.

> **KEY DOCTRINE: Man** >> Man is the special creation of God, made in His own image. He created them male and female as the crowning work of His creation (see Gen. 1:26-30).

How does anger influence your prayer requests? How does anger get in the way of your prayers?

Day 4: Men and women represent God differently.

Read 1 Timothy 2:9-12, identifying Paul's instructions for women.

Paul encouraged women to learn. This exhortation involved a radical departure from the first-century stigma against women and signaled a new freedom for all women who had become Christians. Some scholars see the word *quietly* (see v. 11) as a reference to maintaining a quiet attitude as opposed to a quarrelsome spirit. The phrase "Full submission" (v. 11) emphasized a willingness to be taught and to learn. Paul honored women as teachable members of the church, as capable as men of studying and learning God's Word.

We can identify at least two reasons for Paul's prohibition against women teachers.

1. Within the context of worship, Paul knew the problems posed by false teachers and the temptation for women to misuse their new freedom. Some of the false teachers may have stirred women to claim for themselves a more prominent standing in the church. Paul instructed Timothy not to allow anyone to serve in a leadership position, including newly saved women, who weren't spiritually mature in their faith.

2. The position and influence of a teacher in first-century churches were equated with the office of the pastor, a biblical role for men.

How do men and women represent God differently?

Day 5: Men and women are colaborers with Christ.

Read 1 Timothy 2:13-15, considering Adam's and Eve's roles.

Paul appealed to creation as the theological basis of gender roles (see Gen. 2:18). God established the divine order of male and female before sin entered the world. The fact that Adam was formed first indicated that God placed on Adam a mantle of authority without superiority. Adam's role of leadership didn't mean he was better than Eve. Eve's role of submission didn't mean she was less than Adam.

Paul's final statement appears to suggest salvation for women comes through childbearing. This interpretation would conflict with countless Scripture passages teaching that salvation comes through Christ alone. Paul would never argue that someone can earn salvation through childbearing or any means other than by grace through faith in Christ. Verse 15 was probably meant to affirm roles particular to women, in contrast to those prohibited to them in verses 11-14.

Godly women are mindful of the ways they influence the witness of the church. As men and women carry out the mission of Christ's church, each fulfills a unique, important role. They're colaborers with Christ in taking His gospel mission to the world.

How have you been positively influenced by godly women in your life?

"

True prayer is not a mere mental exercise, nor a vocal performance, but it is deeper far than that—it is spiritual commerce with the Creator of heaven and earth.

CHARLES H. SPURGEON

❯ OBEY THE TEXT

Reflect on the truths found in 1 Timothy 2 and record your responses to the following questions or discuss them with two other members of your Bible-study group.

How does praying for our leaders change our view of them?

What qualities of leadership does God expect faithful men to model?

What does God's call for women to represent Him in the world look like?

MEMORIZE

First of all, then, I urge that petitions, prayers, intercessions, and thanksgivings be made for everyone.

1 TIMOTHY 2:1

MY THOUGHTS

Record insights and questions from this session's group experience
and daily exploration.

_____

_____

_____

_____

_____

_____

_____

MY RESPONSE

Note specific ways you'll put into practice the truth explored this week.

_____

_____

_____

_____

_____

_____

_____

MY PRAYERS

List specific prayer needs and answers to remember this week.

_____

_____

_____

_____

_____

_____

_____

Setting the Example

Godly leaders are needed to lead healthy churches.

1 Timothy 3:1-13

What requirements for church leaders do you value most? Why do you include each requirement?

Organizations rise and fall with leadership. Leaders who reflect the values of the company make a lasting difference. Most of us want our leaders to represent us well. We don't want to see our leaders' names in the news for the wrong reasons. Paul specified high standards for church leaders, knowing their influence would go beyond the local body of believers they served.

❯ UNDERSTAND THE CONTEXT

In 1 Timothy 2 Paul provided instruction to men and women in the church about what they should do and how they should live. In chapter 3 he offered instruction about what church leaders must be and their qualifications for service.

False teachers were creating instability in the church by their spurious doctrine. They were undermining the confidence of believers. Moreover, the false teachers were bringing the gospel into disrepute. The church was floundering and desperately needed godly leadership.

For these reasons Paul addressed the need for qualified individuals to serve as pastors and deacons. First, he expressed God's requirements for overseers. The words *bishop* and *elder* are interchangeable terms for the role of pastor. Paul's requirements didn't give a job description for the pastor, but they indicate the character qualities of a person who would serve in that position (see 1 Tim. 3:1-7; Titus 1:5-9).

In a similar manner, deacons, their wives, and other women who served the church were expected to uphold a high standard of godliness and faithfulness in keeping with their positions (see 1 Tim. 3:8-13).

Paul's qualifications were designed to encourage the right persons to serve and discourage the wrong persons from leadership.

⟩ 1 TIMOTHY 3:1-13

1 This saying is trustworthy: "If anyone aspires to be an **overseer** Ⓐ, he desires a noble work." **2** An overseer, therefore, must be above reproach, the **husband of one wife** Ⓑ, self-controlled, sensible, respectable, hospitable, able to teach, **3** not an excessive drinker, not a bully but gentle, not quarrelsome, not greedy. **4** He must manage his own household competently and have his children under control with all dignity. **5** (If anyone does not know how to manage his own household, how will he take care of God's church?) **6** He must not be a new convert, or he might become conceited and incur the same condemnation as the devil. **7** Furthermore, he must have a good reputation among outsiders, so that he does not fall into disgrace and the devil's trap. **8 Deacons** Ⓒ, likewise, should be worthy of respect, not hypocritical, not drinking a lot of wine, not greedy for money, **9** holding the mystery of the faith with a clear conscience. **10** They must also be **tested first** Ⓓ; if they prove blameless, then they can serve as deacons. **11 Wives** Ⓔ, too, must be worthy of respect, not slanderers, self-controlled, faithful in everything. **12** Deacons are to be husbands of one wife, managing their children and their own households competently. **13** For those who have served well as deacons acquire a good standing for themselves and great boldness in the faith that is in Christ Jesus.

Passage Outline

A Pastor's Heart
(1 Tim. 3:1)

A Pastor's Character
(1 Tim. 3:2-7)

A Deacon's Character
(1 Tim. 3:8-13)

Keywords

Ⓐ This church leader has been called "a bishop" (KJV). The term paints a compelling picture of a person who serves as a pastor today, managing the church's work.

Ⓑ Completely faithful and devoted to the person to whom he is married

Ⓒ Servant leaders or "church helpers" (GNT); the term pictures someone who serves others by running an errand or being a waiter (see 2 Cor. 3:6; Eph. 3:7; Phil. 1:1; Col. 4:7).

Ⓓ Watch them for a while to observe how well they carry out other tasks in the church.

Ⓔ Women aren't excused from living out the standard for servants in the church.

❯ EXPLORE THE TEXT

There's a link between godly pastors and healthy churches. God intended for His churches to have pastors, and He intended for His pastors to meet holy qualifications that reflect His heart. Paul identified this teaching as a trustworthy saying (see 1 Tim. 3:1) because a pastor's life and work are sacred responsibilities that carry eternal implications. The trustworthiness in this context focused on the character and competency of anyone who aspires to be a pastor.

How was Paul's affirmation of the men who desired to be pastors also an affirmation of Timothy?

> **KEY DOCTRINE: The church** >> Although both men and women are gifted for service in the church, the office of pastor is limited to men as qualified by Scripture (see 1 Tim. 3:2).

Spiritual leadership necessitates exemplary behavior. The expression "Above reproach" (v. 2) doesn't indicate sinless perfection. Instead, it depicts the virtuous life of a redeemed individual. A pastor is expected not only to believe and preach the gospel but also to practice it. In significant ways the call to live above reproach is spelled out in Paul's list of behavioral virtues in 1 Timothy 3:1-7.

What dangers do churches face when they compromise these biblical qualifications for leaders?

Paul indicated that it was essential for a potential pastor to have a good reputation among outsiders by living in an undeniably Christlike manner. Otherwise, unbelievers could disparage the name of Christ.

How can you help your pastor consistently exhibit these qualities?

> **BIBLE SKILL: Compare similar passages.** >> Create a list of the qualifications for pastors and deacons listed in 1 Timothy 3. Compare the following passages on biblical expectations for every Christian: Ephesians 5:6-18; Philippians 1:27; 2:14-16; and Colossians 3:5-13. In what ways are the qualifications for pastors and deacons different from the qualities of all believers? How are they similar? Compose a personal statement committing to fulfill scriptural expectations as you serve your church.

The word *deacon* means "one who serves." As Paul had done for pastors, he pointed out the necessity of a Christ-centered home life for a deacon. Like a pastor, a deacon must be a one-woman man, upholding God's ideal for marriage. Furthermore, he must set a worthy example so that his children can clearly comprehend the way a godly man lives. Paul reminded deacons of their spiritual rewards for serving well.

How does faithful service honor God?

› APPLY THE TEXT

> › Believers must consider what role God desires them to play in their local church.

> › Believers can affirm men who demonstrate the qualities of a faithful pastor.

> › Believers should seek to live a life that honors God through service.

Spend time praying about the role you play in your church. Ask God to help you faithfully serve in that role. Are there other roles He may be asking you to consider? What keeps you from taking on an additional role?

Discuss ways your group can encourage your pastor and his family. What actions should be taken as a result of this discussion?

List ways you honor the Lord both within and outside your church. What actions will you take this week to honor Him in your church? List actions you'll take to honor Him outside the church.

❯ DAILY EXPLORATION

Day 1: To serve as a pastor is an honorable calling.

Read 1 Timothy 3:1, considering what it means to be called to be a pastor.

Aspiring to be a spiritual leader is worthwhile, but there can be a big gap between aspiration and qualification. Therefore, Paul emphasized the qualifications for serving as a pastor. The word *overseer* described a pastor as someone who directs and oversees the church's ministry. Throughout the New Testament the terms *pastor*, *overseer*, *elder*, and *bishop* are used synonymously.

Paul reminded Timothy that serving as a pastor is "a noble work." It's an honorable calling from God that requires an honorable life as a testimony to His grace. To represent the Savior in the task of spreading the gospel and leading His church is a rigorous responsibility that should never be regarded lightly. A pastor's heart must beat in rhythm with the Savior's mission while leading believers to reach the unsaved and to disciple the saved.

Why is it important for you to seriously consider the role God wants you to play in His work?

Day 2: A pastor must hold key biblical qualifications.

Read 1 Timothy 3:2-3, noting the requirements for a pastor.

The first key virtue that Paul listed as important for a pastor is marital fidelity. This requirement refers to a man who's faithfully and unquestionably devoted to his wife and whose covenant of marriage presents a magnetic witness for Christ. Verse 2 lists five more essential characteristics. *Self-controlled* points to a man with the ability to refrain from making rash decisions or living irresponsibly. *Sensible* describes someone who's reasonable in human interactions. A person who lives in this manner is *respectable*. Being *hospitable* includes the practice of welcoming others into the home and the attitude of cordiality. The phrase "able to teach" refers to someone who possesses a Spirit-endowed gift to connect with listeners and to impart Scripture in a manner that enables them to understand and apply God's message. A pastor should have the ability to communicate God's Word by effectively explaining doctrinal truths and skillfully refuting heretical ideas.

Four additional character qualities are listed in verse 3. Each one is stated as a prohibition to emphasize behavior a pastor should avoid: "not an excessive drinker, not a bully but gentle, not quarrelsome, and not greedy."

What dangers do churches face when they compromise on these biblical qualifications for leaders?

Day 3: A pastor must be spiritually mature.

Read 1 Timothy 3:4-7, understanding the importance of leading well at home.

The word *manage* (see v. 4) denotes the exercise of discipline and authority, immersed in compassion. When a pastor leads well on the home front, he demonstrates that he can take care of God's church. By modeling integrity on a small scale in a family, a pastor proves his capability of spiritual leadership on a larger scale like a church.

Pride is an obstacle for any Christian but can be especially problematic for a pastor. Consequently, Paul argued that the pastor "must not be a new convert" (v. 6). A believer needs a certain level of biblical knowledge and spiritual maturity before assuming the role of pastor.

What insights have you gained from Paul's detailed list of qualifications for being a pastor? How do these also apply to your life and witness for God?

Day 4: Deacons must also meet biblical qualifications.

Read 1 Timothy 3:8-12, reviewing the qualifications for a deacon.

A deacon's character must "be worthy of respect" (v. 8). This expression combines the idea of earnestness and dignity. A deacon must not be hypocritical. He can't present a righteous image at church while behaving like an unbeliever outside church. Deacons, like pastors, should also be known for their self-control in regard to drinking and money. A deacon should hold firmly "the mystery of the faith" in Christ (v. 9). The word *holding* means not only to possess but also to preserve. The word *mystery* refers to truths previously hidden but now revealed through Christ. A deacon also shouldn't be placed his role hastily but should "be tested first" (v. 10). To be tested involves an observation and examination of belief and behavior. The general evaluation of being proved blameless mirrors the pastor's qualification to be so irreproachable in ethical demeanor that no charge against him could be proved legitimate.

Whether Paul referred to the wives of deacons or women in general is unclear. Because he was addressing deacons, the context suggests that Paul had in mind deacons' wives. Nevertheless, the application applies to every woman in the church. Four requirements are needed.

1. She's to be worthy of respect. Godly behavior is to be expected of all church members, regardless of role or gender.

2. She's to avoid being an accuser or slanderer. The word *slanderers* is derived from a word designating the devil, who makes false accusations.

3. She must be self-controlled.

4. In summary, she must be "faithful in everything" (v. 11), whether in her family or in her service in the church. *Reliable* is an appropriate synonym for *faithful.*

In what ways are the qualifications for a deacon similar to those for a pastor?

Day 5: Serving well reaps spiritual rewards.

Read 1 Timothy 3:13, identifying the rewards for serving well.

It's quite likely that false teachers in Ephesus had weakened respect for church leaders and their roles. Consequently, Paul reminded deacons about their spiritual rewards for serving well.

1. They acquire good standing. When a deacon serves the Lord and the church in an exemplary manner, other believers recognize his dedication and sacrifice. As a result, he's esteemed as a person with an honorable reputation.

2. They receive "great boldness in the faith" that comes from Christ Jesus. Deep devotion to the Lord assures deacons that Jesus is worthy of their best service. It stirs a greater level of confidence in the power of Jesus to overcome any obstacle. Not only deacons but all believers who live honorably for the Lord develop an ever-growing boldness in the faith.

How could memorizing 1 Timothy 3:13 help you remember the importance of Christian service?

The way to gain a good reputation is to endeavor to be what you desire to appear.

SOCRATES

> OBEY THE TEXT

Reflect on the truths found in 1 Timothy 3 and record your responses to the following questions or discuss them with two other members of your Bible-study group.

Because pastors are held in such high regard, should every Christian aspire to join a church staff?

Understanding the importance Scripture assigns to these positions, how much care should a church invest when selecting leaders?

How should we apply the detailed references to the wives of church leaders in church life?

MEMORIZE

Those who have served well as deacons acquire
a good standing for themselves and great boldness
in the faith that is in Christ Jesus.

1 TIMOTHY 3:13

MY THOUGHTS

Record insights and questions from this session's group experience and daily exploration.

_____

_____

_____

_____

_____

_____

_____

MY RESPONSE

Note specific ways you'll put into practice the truth explored this week.

_____

_____

_____

_____

_____

_____

_____

_____

MY PRAYERS

List specific prayer needs and answers to remember this week.

_____

_____

_____

_____

_____

_____

_____

Staying on Course

Believers must be nourished on God's Word so that they'll know the truth.

1 Timothy 4:1-13

Have you ever been the victim of a scam or false advertisement? After that experience how did you respond to "can't miss" claims?

Our world is filled with scam artists and people who bend the truth for their own benefit. We should carefully examine the claims people make, especially when they want access to our money. In the same way, the devil sells beliefs and behaviors that either deny or twist the message of the gospel. It's imperative for followers of Christ to be aware of distorted beliefs and deceptive doctrines. We must be equipped by God's Word and stay the course of true faith.

❯ UNDERSTAND THE CONTEXT

Paul wrote this letter while visiting Macedonia. He had left Timothy in Ephesus to help the church gain more solid ground in Christian living and doctrine. Although Paul hoped to rejoin Timothy soon (see 1 Tim. 3:14), he knew much needed to be done in the meantime. He wanted the believers to know how to conduct themselves not only *in* church but also *as* the church (see v. 15).

Paul knew both right behavior and right belief were vital as the church encountered opposition. In chapter 4 he warned Timothy about the false teachers who would not only arise in the later times but were already afflicting believers in Ephesus. Hypocritically demanding of others what they wouldn't endure themselves, these phony prophets claimed to be defenders of the Jewish law. In reality they were subverters of both law and grace.

Paul saw Timothy as his son in the ministry and, as such, wanted him to succeed as "a good servant of Christ Jesus" (4:6). Rather than indulging in speculation and myths, Timothy's teaching was to focus on godliness so that people would place their hope securely in Christ alone.

Timothy had a gift for preaching and teaching, but Paul didn't leave him in Ephesus merely to teach the church. He wanted Timothy to be an example of how to live for Christ (see v. 12). Timothy was to give careful attention to his life and his teaching. Persevering in both would benefit not only his hearers but also himself.

➤ 1 TIMOTHY 4:1-13

1 Now the Spirit explicitly says that in later times some will depart from the faith, paying attention to **deceitful spirits** Ⓐ and the teachings of demons, **2** through the hypocrisy of liars whose **consciences are seared** Ⓑ. **3** They forbid marriage and demand abstinence from foods that God created to be received with gratitude by those who believe and know the truth. **4** For everything created by God is good, and nothing is to be rejected if it is received with thanksgiving, **5** since it is sanctified by the word of God and by prayer.
6 If you point these things out to the brothers and sisters, you will be a good servant of Christ Jesus, nourished by the words of the faith and the good teaching that you have followed. **7** But have nothing to do with pointless and silly myths. Rather, train yourself in godliness. **8** For the **training of the body** Ⓒ has limited benefit, but **godliness** Ⓓ is beneficial in every way, since it holds promise for the present life and also for the life to come. **9** This saying is trustworthy and deserves full acceptance. **10** For this reason we labor and strive, because we have put our hope in the living God, who is the **Savior** Ⓔ of all people, especially of those who believe. **11** Command and teach these things.
12 Don't let anyone despise your youth, but set an example for the believers in speech, in conduct, in love, in faith, and in purity. **13** Until I come, give your attention to public reading, exhortation, and teaching.

Passage Outline

Be Aware
(1 Tim. 4:1-5)

Be Disciplined
(1 Tim. 4:6-10)

Be an Example
(1 Tim. 4:11-13)

Keywords

Ⓐ They would be told lies from demonic influences that would fool them.

Ⓑ The word for *seared* in the original language calls to mind a hot iron branding the skin, leaving it numb and insensitive. The liars would feel nothing at all for the people they were deceiving.

Ⓒ Getting the body physically fit

Ⓓ Seeking to live in the center of God's will, Paul often prioritized godliness in his letters to Timothy (see 1 Tim. 2:2; 3:16; 4:7-8; 6:3,5-6; 2 Tim. 3:5). Growing in godliness requires believers to engage in daily spiritual exercise.

Ⓔ Paul affirmed that God is our Savior, or Deliverer (see 1 Tim. 1:1; 2:3; Titus 1:3; 2:10).

❯ EXPLORE THE TEXT

Paul understood that the world is a battlefield between truth and falsehood. He affirmed that in the later times—a period that began with Jesus' first coming and will conclude with His second coming—it would be necessary to practice discernment. Paul emphasized two reasons people would depart from the faith: (1) They would pay attention to deceitful spirits. (2) They would embrace the teachings of demons.

False teachers were promoting behavior that denied God's purpose for marriage and food. The false teachers promoted a legalism that minimized God's grace and maximized human rules.

How does sin desensitize a person to truth? What other factors might desensitize a person to truth?

> **BIBLE SKILL: Compare passages that use the same word or phrase. >>**
> To understand the term "later times" (1 Tim. 4:1), compare Paul's description in verses 1-4 with the following passages: 2 Timothy 3:1-9; 2 Thessalonians 2:3-12; 2 Peter 3:3-7; and Jude 18-19. Summarize what you discover. Then compare the previous passages with Hebrews 1:1-3. How does this comparison add to your understanding of later times? How does your concept affect your daily decisions and conduct of life?

Paul wanted Timothy to mix tenderness into serious warnings. He especially wanted Timothy to be a good servant of the Lord by demonstrating discipline in his life and teaching. To accomplish that lofty goal, Timothy needed to practice two disciplines: (1) He needed to be nourished by the words of the faith. (2) He needed to feed on good teaching, or doctrine.

Paul made it clear that a compromise between truth and falsehood wasn't acceptable. Paul urged Timothy to train himself in godliness. Paul believed both physical and spiritual discipline are valuable, but Timothy must prioritize godliness as a discipline that matters both now and forever.

What makes godliness a difficult discipline to develop and practice?

The best way for Timothy to deflect complaints was to set an example for the other believers, beginning with his speech. Paul expected Timothy to speak with Christ-centered authority while avoiding words that could stir strife and alienation. In addition, Timothy's conduct was to be exemplary. Love is the unmistakable mark of an exemplary spiritual leader, and Paul wanted Timothy to walk in it. Faith was essential for Timothy's leadership in a culture of unbelief. His bold trust would serve as a model for other struggling seekers. Moreover, Timothy needed to pursue purity. For the sake of the gospel, his life needed to be morally beyond reproach.

In what ways could you be an example for other believers, beginning in your home?

❯ APPLY THE TEXT

> ❯ Believers must be aware that false teachers will try to lead them astray.

> ❯ Believers must be disciplined in their lives, seeking to honor God by living out the gospel.

> ❯ Believers must remain focused on God's Word to be examples of godly living.

How can your vigilance be strengthened as you learn about false teaching and heresy?

Discuss as a group ways of engaging one another in discussions about theology, including false doctrines. How can the group detect false teachings?

Reflect on 1 Timothy 4:13. List one action you can take in each of the three areas Paul instructed Timothy to focus on.

❯ DAILY EXPLORATION

Day 1: There will be false teachers.

Read 1 Timothy 4:1-2, noting what the Holy Spirit says will occur in later times.

Paul affirmed that in later times, Christians would need to practice discernment. He knew this fact because the Holy Spirit had made it clear. Jesus taught that false prophets would "rise up and deceive many" (Matt. 24:11), and the Holy Spirit confirmed that "some will depart from the faith" (1 Tim. 4:1). The verb *depart* signifies a defection from someone or something. It involves a willful abandonment of truth. Jesus used this same verb in the parable about the soils to describe people who "believe for a while and fall away in a time of testing" (Luke 8:13). Although the devil initiates toxic, demonic teaching, it comes through humans. Paul characterized people who transmit such teaching as "liars whose consciences are seared" (1 Tim. 4:2). Their deadly lies are cloaked by a hypocritical mask of sincerity.

This passage doesn't contradict the security of a believer. Paul's warning to Timothy reflects an awareness that some people who claim to be followers of Christ have a spurious faith camouflaged in religious works. Accordingly, their faith rested in their own rules of righteousness instead of the righteousness of Christ.

Has has sin desensitized you to truth? What other factors might desensitize you to truth?

Day 2: Believers can delight in the goodness of God's creation.

Read 1 Timothy 4:3-5, considering the good things God has created.

Some of the teachers in Ephesus were influenced by the idea that spiritual things were morally good, but physical things were morally bad. In a misguided effort to achieve a higher spiritual status, they labeled marriage and marital intimacy as sinful. God never commends an activity that contradicts or compromises His stated purpose as revealed in Scripture. God ordained marriage between a man and a woman from the beginning of creation, and His blessing on it continues. Celibacy mandated by human rules can't produce righteousness.

Paul emphasized not only that the false teachers were wrong about their food restrictions but also that those foods were created by God and should be "received with gratitude" (v. 3). Rather than deny the goodness of God's creation, believers can delight in it and enjoy it as God intended. This truth, however, isn't a license to abuse the things God has created for our pleasure. Food can be eaten for pleasure and nutrition, but gluttony is an abuse. God blesses sexual intimacy in marriage, but adultery and pornography are abuses of His gift.

Why is the reminder that God gives us good things tied to warnings about false teachers?

Day 3: Believers should discipline themselves in godliness.

Read 1 Timothy 4:6-10, comparing physical training with godly training.

Training doesn't happen by chance or coincidence. It's a deliberate discipline and commitment to a focused goal. Training in godliness involves both attitude and action, belief and behavior. The Greek word translated *train* (see v. 7) is related to the word *gymnasium*. Paul used that word to reinforce spiritual exercise as an essential aspect of Timothy's role as a godly leader. In order to lead well *for* Christ, Timothy was to learn well *from* Christ. Learning involves spiritual training. Spiritual training involves the exercise of rigorous devotion. The exercise of rigorous devotion leads to an effective impact for Christ.

To develop godliness, believers must "labor and strive" (v. 10). We don't labor to earn God's favor but rather because we've received God's grace. The word *strive* carries an athletic meaning, referring to the agony involved in a contest. Paul was emphasizing that living a godly life isn't a leisurely stroll down easy street. It requires an agonizing struggle against sin and Satan.

How does the commitment to discipline yourself in godliness fit into your priorities?

Day 4: Age doesn't disqualify a believer from leading.

Read 1 Timothy 4:11-12, paying attention to the instructions for all believers, regardless of age.

Paul gave Timothy a robust challenge to "command and teach these things" (v. 11). *Command* was a strong word for directing others with authority. *Teach* was the customary word for transmitting information that could be applied.

Timothy may have been reluctant to command and teach the church in Ephesus because of his young age. First-century culture valued the aged. An older teacher was generally considered wiser and more knowledgeable than a young teacher. Paul wanted Timothy not to allow anyone to belittle his ministry simply because he was relatively young (though Timothy may have been at least thirty years old).

Paul's admonition that no one should despise Timothy's youth served as a twofold encouragement.

1. It personally affirmed Timothy.

2. It communicated to the believers that Paul had left Timothy in charge as overseer. Age doesn't disqualify either the young or the old from leading.

If you're younger, how can you gain the respect of a more mature audience? If you're older, how can you be more open to respecting people who are younger than you?

Day 5: All believers should focus on God's Word.

Read 1 Timothy 4:13, identifying what believers should focus on while waiting.

Until Paul could visit, Timothy was to give attention to three areas of ministry.

1. *The public reading of Scripture.* This would have included the Old Testament Scriptures and the letters of Paul that were circulating among the churches.

2. *The exhortation of God's Word.* This form of preaching urged listeners to apply the truth of Scripture.

3. *Teaching believers to understand the essential doctrines and fundamental elements of the faith.* Paul expected Timothy to focus his attention on God's Word. Like Timothy, all believers must remain focused on God's Word.

> **KEY DOCTRINE: Scripture** >> The Bible reveals the principles by which God judges us and therefore is and will remain to the end of the world the true center of Christian union and the supreme standard by which all human conduct, creeds, and religious opinions should be tried (see Ps. 19:7-10).

How can you use God's Word to nourish your soul?

Every day that we are not practicing godliness we are being conformed to the world of ungodliness around us.

JERRY BRIDGES

❯ OBEY THE TEXT

Reflect on the truths found in 1 Timothy 4 and record your responses to the following questions or discuss them with two other members of your Bible-study group.

Why should we take very seriously people who promote false teachings?

What makes the spiritual comparison to physical training such an apt analogy for contemporary life?

How should we measure our spiritual progress?

MEMORIZE

Until I come, give your attention to public reading, exhortation, and teaching.

1 TIMOTHY 4:13

MY THOUGHTS

Record insights and questions from this session's group experience
and daily exploration.

MY RESPONSE

Note specific ways you'll put into practice the truth explored this week.

MY PRAYERS

List specific prayer needs and answers to remember this week.

Being Responsible

Believers should care for others, including widows and ministers.

1 Timothy 5:1-8,17-21

What role should the church play in caring for the needs of people in the community?

Most of us realize that a church isn't a shrine for morally perfect people. It's full of people like you and me, who are often messy, careless, confused, selfish, and desperately in need of forgiveness and correction. With all of our relational challenges, we sometimes fail to minister and communicate respectfully and mercifully. Thankfully, God provides clear instructions about how to treat people in needy situations and pastors in leadership.

❯ UNDERSTAND **THE CONTEXT**

Paul's desire to see the church in Ephesus thrive is obvious from the details he gave Timothy. As a young pastor, Timothy faced a steep learning curve. Paul offered him guidance about several significant matters. The first involved advice for relating to a wide age range of church members (see 1 Tim. 5:1-2). Paul wanted Timothy to give gentle correction to an elderly believer, as if pleading with a father. On the other end of the age spectrum, Paul advised Timothy to lead younger men as brothers. Similarly with women, Paul instructed Timothy to approach older women tenderly as mothers and to treat younger women respectfully as sisters.

Paul also gave Timothy instructions about caring for widows (see vv. 3-16). He pointed out that believers have a responsibility to care for a widowed family member, while widows without family support need help from the church. Some widows, however, don't qualify for church support.

Given that the immediately preceding context deals with widows, we could easily think Paul's instructions in verses 17-21 involved older men. However, this section specifically refers to people who preach and teach. Paul outlined several ways Timothy and the church should relate to these spiritual leaders, including how to deal with pastors who had been accused of wrongdoing.

In verses 22-23 Paul interjected personal instructions for Timothy. Because of Timothy's health problems, Paul advised him to mix some wine with the water he typically drank.

In the opening verses of chapter 6, Paul offered guidance for the way believing servants and masters should relate to each other. In all of these relationships, Paul emphasized responsible behavior that honored the Lord.

❯ 1 TIMOTHY 5:1-8,17-21

1 Don't rebuke an older man, but **exhort** Ⓐ him as a father, younger men as brothers, **2** older women as mothers, and the younger women as sisters with all purity. **3** Support **widows** Ⓑ who are genuinely in need. **4** But if any widow has children or grandchildren, let them learn to practice godliness toward their own family first and to **repay their parents** Ⓒ, for this pleases God. **5** The widow who is truly in need and left all alone has put her hope in God and continues night and day in her petitions and prayers; **6** however, she who is **self-indulgent** Ⓓ is dead even while she lives. **7** Command this also, so that they will be above reproach. **8** But if anyone does not provide for his own family, especially for his own household, he has denied the faith and is worse than an unbeliever.

17 The **elders** Ⓔ who are good leaders are to be considered worthy of double honor, especially those who work hard at preaching and teaching. **18** For the Scripture says: "Do not muzzle an ox while it is treading out the grain," and **"The worker is worthy of his wages."** Ⓕ **19** Don't accept an accusation against an elder unless it is supported by two or three witnesses. **20** Publicly rebuke those who sin, so that the rest will be afraid. **21** I solemnly charge you before God and Christ Jesus and the elect angels to observe these things without prejudice, doing nothing out of favoritism.

Passage Outline

Respect All
(1 Tim. 5:1-2)

Care for Widows
(1 Tim. 5:3-8)

Care for Pastors
(1 Tim. 5:17-21)

Keywords

Ⓐ Make an appeal or plea in a respectful way.

Ⓑ Paul expressed his concern that widows be shown respect and receive the help they needed. James also directed believers to care for widows (see Jas. 1:27). Luke showed that caring for widows mattered to Jesus (see Luke 4:25-26; 20:47; 21:2-3).

Ⓒ They serve God by helping their parents, as their parents helped them when they were children.

Ⓓ She lives only to please herself, because seeking selfish pleasure matters most of all to her.

Ⓔ Church leaders

Ⓕ Jesus' teaching from Luke 10:7

> EXPLORE THE TEXT

As a young pastor, Timothy faced the challenge of leading men and women of various ages. Paul knew part of Timothy's leadership involved confronting unacceptable attitudes and actions among believers.

How does the way we approach people affect their willingness to listen? How can a person balance sternness and love?

Paul impressed on Timothy not only the responsibility of caring for widows but also effectively managing ministry on their behalf. The children or grandchildren of a widow were expected to care for her needs. By taking responsibility for her well-being, they would practice godliness and provide tangible proof of their devotion to Christ. The demonstration of godliness and compassion within the family context authenticates three attributes: genuine faith, gratitude toward a mother or grandmother, and pleasing service to the Lord.

Where's the line between family expectations and church responsibility? How can believers balance their responsibilities for both?

BIBLE SKILL: **Compare similar passages.** >> Read 1 Timothy 5:9-16 and record Paul's requirements for widows who received church benevolence. Read the article on widows in *Holman Illustrated Bible Dictionary* or in a similar resource. Compare this article and Paul's instructions for ministry to widows with the following Scriptures: Deuteronomy 10:18; 24:20-21; 26:12-13. Based on what you read, what could your church do to fulfill scriptural expectations for ministry to widows in your church?

Pastors in Ephesus, like pastors today, had an obligation to fulfill their calling from God. Consequently, pastors who are good leaders should be considered worthy of financial support. Paul called attention to pastors who work hard at preaching and teaching because the task of effectively communicating the gospel is a labor-intensive ministry.

Do you believe it's more difficult or easier to lead a church today than it was thirty years ago? Give examples to illustrate your response.

All pastors are flawed individuals. None are above criticism, and none are beyond being falsely accused. Some accusations may be legitimate and require examination. Other accusations can be spurious and arise from impure motives that require rejection. Timothy was charged with the responsibility of confronting the guilty people and making sure any investigations of wrongdoing were conducted without prejudice or favoritism. No one was to receive special treatment. The rebuke was to be balanced with grace.

What factors can make a pastor or another church leader an easy target for a false accusation? How can a church practice the actions Paul called for?

❯ APPLY **THE TEXT**

> ❯ Believers are to treat one another as respected family members.

> ❯ Believers are to help take care of the needs of faithful believers who face life alone.

> ❯ Believers are responsible to God for the support they provide their pastoral leadership.

As a group, identify principles from today's study for addressing sensitive matters with one another. What actions need to be implemented as a result of this discussion?

Reflect on the responsibilities you have for others as a member of a family and a church. What actions do you need to take to better care for the people in your family and in your church who are unable to care for themselves?

Memorize 1 Timothy 5:25. Consider ways you can express gratitude and generosity to your pastoral leaders. What actions do you need to take to encourage your pastor and church leaders?

❯ DAILY EXPLORATION

Day 1: Honor others regardless of age or gender.

Read 1 Timothy 5:1-2, looking for the guidelines Paul gave to Timothy.

Paul gave Timothy two guidelines for relating to elderly men: (1) Paul instructed Timothy not to engage in verbal rage toward a senior believer. Contempt for a member of God's family must be rejected. (2) A mature man was to be exhorted as a father who deserves respect. Such an approach would uphold Timothy's role of pastoral leadership and would reduce relational friction.

Similarly, Paul reminded Timothy to engage younger men as if they were his beloved brothers. Timothy needed to treat them with respect and affection. When they needed correction, he was expected to give it without pompous censure.

Likewise, Paul offered two guidelines for Timothy to follow as he ministered to women in Ephesus: (1) Timothy was to relate to older women as mothers. (2) Paul wanted Timothy to treat younger women as sisters. Specifically, Timothy was to maintain a standard of purity and to avoid sexual immorality. By viewing the opposite sex as members of God's family, Timothy would provide healthy, holy leadership. When confrontation was necessary, Timothy was to carry it out in a manner that honored both older and younger women in the church.

How might the way you approach people affect their willingness to listen?

Day 2: Support the needy.

Read 1 Timothy 5:3-4, considering the call to take care of widows.

The Old Testament prominently emphasizes caring for widows (see Ex. 22:22; Deut. 24:17,19; Ps. 68:5; Isa. 1:17). Apparently, the burden of caregiving had strained the congregation in Ephesus, necessitating clarification about the qualifications for support. Although our English word *widow* refers to a woman whose husband has died, the Greek word for *widow* describes a woman who may have lost her husband by death, incarceration, or desertion. Some widows had financial resources that had been left to them by their deceased husbands. Some received support from their extended families. Widows who were destitute and without family support for daily provisions were classified as true widows who needed help from the church.

> KEY DOCTRINE: **The Christian and the social order** >> All Christians should work to provide for the orphaned, the needy, the abused, the aged, the helpless, and the sick (see Col. 3:12-17).

How does the care of widows in a church serve as a testimony of Christ in the larger community?

Day 3: Use discernment in helping the needy.

Read 1 Timothy 5:5-8, noting the distinctions Paul explained.

In contrast to the widows who genuinely needed support, Paul implied that some widows didn't qualify for church support. This was especially true for a widow who's self-indulgent. She's described as being "dead even while she lives" (v. 6).

Paul was establishing the case for discernment and wisdom in utilizing church resources for widows. To support a widow who clearly traveled the path of self-indulgence would not only represent unwise stewardship but would also enable the widow to continue in her sin. Paul expected Timothy to teach the congregation and warn the widows. If the congregation would honor and support the true widows, if the widows would avoid sinful behavior, and if family members would act responsibly toward a widowed mother or grandmother, neither the widows nor the church could be blamed for negligence or impropriety. Furthermore, the gospel wouldn't be discredited.

Why do you suppose Paul spelled out such detailed instruction for the care of widows?

Day 4: Support church leaders.

Read 1 Timothy 5:17-18, contemplating the comparison between the elders and the ox.

In these verses Paul was referring to pastors who have the responsibility of overseeing church ministries and preaching the gospel. Pastors in Ephesus, like pastors today, had an obligation to fulfill their calling from God. Consequently, pastors who are good leaders should be considered worthy of financial support and should be treated with respect. Paul called attention to pastors who work hard at preaching and teaching because the task of effectively communicating the gospel is a labor-intensive ministry. The twin tasks, when done effectively, are worthy of financial support and respect.

Paul quoted from the Old Testament to support his instruction. The command "Do not muzzle an ox while it is treading out the grain" (v. 18) was found in the Mosaic law and pertained to the care of oxen while they threshed grain (see Deut. 25:4). Muzzling the oxen prevented them from enjoying some of the grain. They were to be allowed the opportunity to eat because of their work and their worth to the owner. Paul's point was that pastors should be sufficiently compensated for their work in the gospel and their worth to the Savior's mission. Paul also cited Jesus' words "The worker is worthy of his wages" (v. 18; see Matt. 10:10). If a laboring ox was rewarded for its work, a pastor should be supported for his labor.

Do you believe it's more difficult or easier to lead a church today than it was thirty years ago? Why?

Day 5: Handle conflict appropriately.

Read 1 Timothy 5:19-21, taking note of Paul's instructions.

Paul was well aware that conflicts are common in churches. He personally understood the emotional agony and the damage resulting from false accusations. Paul wasn't advocating preferential treatment for pastors. He was recommending fair and unbiased examination. Consequently, he urged the rejection of unsubstantiated charges against a pastor. The danger existed that slander could discredit the integrity of a leader's life and could damage the ministry in Ephesus. Such accusations against a pastor weren't to be received without clear and warranted corroboration.

The condition for accepting charges must be based on the testimonies of "two or three witnesses" (v. 19). Paul supported his instruction by grounding it in the Old Testament stipulation that multiple witnesses were necessary to consider an accusation (see Deut. 17:6; 19:15). When the charges are received, a thorough investigation of the allegation can be conducted, and evidence can be presented.

What factors can make a pastor or another church leader an easy target for a false accusation?

Giving is the secret to a healthy life. Not necessarily money, but whatever a person has to give of encouragement, sympathy, and understanding.

JOHN D. ROCKEFELLER JR.

❯ OBEY **THE TEXT**

Reflect on the truths found in 1 Timothy 5 and record your responses to the following questions or discuss them with two other members of your Bible-study group.

What age and gender distinctions do we find in 1 Timothy 5 that we should apply to our workplace or community?

What do Paul's stern words for negligent family members tell you about how seriously God takes these relationships?

How can we know whether we're meeting our obligations to the people God has entrusted to our care?

MEMORIZE

Good works are obvious, and those that are not obvious cannot remain hidden.

1 TIMOTHY 5:25

MY THOUGHTS

Record insights and questions from this session's group experience and daily exploration.

_____

_____

_____

_____

_____

_____

_____

MY RESPONSE

Note specific ways you'll put into practice the truth explored this week.

_____

_____

_____

_____

_____

_____

_____

MY PRAYERS

List specific prayer needs and answers to remember this week.

_____

_____

_____

_____

_____

_____

_____

Lasting Investments

Believers should be motivated by the value of living a godly life, as opposed to material gain.

1 Timothy 6:6-19

What was your first job? What did you like most about it? Would you want to do that kind of work again? Explain.

Most of us got our first jobs not because we wanted that particular job but because we wanted the paycheck that came with it. It wasn't a career choice but something we could do until we found a job that promised a bigger paycheck. Nothing is wrong with wanting a job that pays well. The problem is knowing how to define "pays well." Money is a useful servant but must not become a master over our thoughts and actions.

❯ UNDERSTAND THE CONTEXT

In chapter 6 Paul closed his letter to Timothy with words of wisdom about money, helping Timothy address the traps that come when people base their lives and self-worth on possessions. He restated the necessity of confronting and correcting the false teachings that had infiltrated the church. He pointed out that the false teachers' thinking was corrupt and conceited. They promoted a false doctrine of prosperity as a means of godliness. They craved material gain and lusted for wealth. Their teaching carried perilous implications for the church.

In response to the false teachers' greed, Paul issued a warning about the snare of wealth and the danger it holds for plunging people into ruin. He explained that the love of money is a root of evil and can lure believers "away from the faith" (v. 10).

After addressing the danger of materialism, Paul urged Timothy to avoid false doctrines and to flee from the enticements of harmful desire. He told him to pursue holy virtues and to fight for the faith. Paul expected Timothy to proclaim and protect the gospel and to boldly live the life to which he was called. He reminded Timothy about the confession of faith he had made "in the presence of many witnesses" (v. 12), encouraging him to faithfully persevere in the challenging culture of Ephesus.

Paul cited two reasons for Timothy to continue leading the church:

1. The glorious return of Christ

2. The immeasurable attributes of God

Because Ephesus was a key center for the worship of the Roman emperor, Paul deliberately contrasted the worship of a human leader with the worship of the peerless Ruler of the universe who's the Lord of all people and all worldly leaders.

Paul urged wealthy believers to avoid arrogance and elitism. He challenged them to use their wealth generously for good goals and to leverage their stewardship for eternal dividends.

➤ 1 TIMOTHY 6:6-19

6 Godliness with **contentment** Ⓐ is great gain. **7** For we brought nothing into the world, and we can take nothing out. **8** If we have food and clothing, we will be content with these. **9** But those who want to be rich fall into temptation, a trap, and many **foolish and harmful desires** Ⓑ, which plunge people into ruin and destruction. **10** For the love of money is a root of all kinds of evil, and by craving it, some have wandered away from the faith and pierced themselves with many griefs. **11** But you, man of God, flee from these things, and pursue righteousness, godliness, faith, love, endurance, and gentleness. **12** Fight the good fight of the faith. Take hold of eternal life to which you were **called** Ⓒ and about which you have **made a good confession** Ⓓ in the presence of many witnesses. **13** In the presence of God, who gives life to all, and of Christ Jesus, who gave a good confession before **Pontius Pilate** Ⓔ, I charge you **14** to keep this command without fault or failure until the appearing of our Lord Jesus Christ. **15** God will bring this about in his own time. He is the blessed and only Sovereign, the King of kings, and the Lord of lords, **16** who alone is immortal and who lives in unapproachable light, whom no one has seen or can see, to him be honor and eternal power. Amen. **17** Instruct those who are rich in the present age not to be arrogant or to set their hope on the uncertainty of wealth, but on God, who richly provides us with all things to enjoy. **18** Instruct them to do what is good, to be rich in good works, to be generous and willing to share, **19** storing up treasure for themselves as a good foundation for the coming age, so that they may take hold of what is truly life.

Passage Outline

True Contentment
(1 Tim. 6:6-10)

True Riches
(1 Tim. 6:11-16)

Stewards of Good Works
(1 Tim. 6:17-19)

Keywords

Ⓐ Meaning sufficiency or a sense that we need nothing more. Paul used *content* when he described what the Lord had taught him about how to live with wealth or in poverty (see Phil. 4:11).

Ⓑ Paul consistently warned believers about fleshly, worldly desires (see Rom. 1:24; 6:12; 13:14; Gal. 5:16,24).

Ⓒ Invited by God to live out his faith and God's plan (see 1 Cor. 1:9; 1 Pet. 2:9)

Ⓓ Timothy clearly testified that he had given his life to Christ.

Ⓔ The Roman governor of Judea who interrogated Jesus and gave the order to crucify Him (see Mark 15:1-5,15)

❯ EXPLORE THE TEXT

Paul warned against greed and a dependence on wealth for security. He reminded Timothy that true contentment can be found only in godliness. Lasting contentment has nothing to do with material wealth or worldly success. The slippery slope of greed starts as a temptation, becomes a trap, then ultimately turns into a tragedy. The matter of money is indeed a matter of the heart. The love of money and a craving for riches are symptomatic of a heart that puts its trust in a currency that God doesn't accept. A love of money erects an idol in the heart that exalts itself above God's sufficiency.

What does it mean to base our contentment on Christ?

Timothy was commanded to flee from the lust for money, the lure of heretical doctrines, and the liability of quarreling about trivial matters in the church. Timothy was not only to flee from harmful things but also to pursue holy things: "righteousness, godliness, faith, love, endurance, and gentleness" (1 Tim. 6:11).

How would the pursuits Paul identified in verse 11 counter greed?

Elsewhere Paul stressed the intense spiritual battle faced by every follower of Christ (see Eph. 6:11). Spiritual warfare requires believers to put on the full armor of God. "The good fight" (1 Tim. 6:12) described the praiseworthy nature of the contest as Timothy contended for the faith. His assignment involved wrestling against the false teachers for purity of doctrine. Paul urged Timothy to fulfill his calling because he was accountable to God, "who gives life to all" (v. 13). Timothy was expected to labor in the harvest and to avoid speculation about the timing of the second coming, which will occur according to God's timetable. In view of Christ's return, Paul's writing erupted in majestic praise to God. He expressed several attributes of God's greatness that would motivate Timothy's service.

How does focusing on Jesus and His character help a believer fulfill God's purposes?

Paul said affluent believers should strive for two goals: (1) They should be "rich in good works" (v. 18). Material wealth can be used to bless others and spread the gospel. (2) They should strive "to be generous and willing to share" (v. 18). Paul knew wise stewardship of all possessions is an eternal investment.

In what ways can believers leverage their financial resources to spread the gospel and strengthen the church?

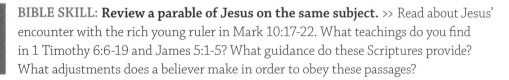

BIBLE SKILL: **Review a parable of Jesus on the same subject.** >> Read about Jesus' encounter with the rich young ruler in Mark 10:17-22. What teachings do you find in 1 Timothy 6:6-19 and James 5:1-5? What guidance do these Scriptures provide? What adjustments does a believer make in order to obey these passages?

› APPLY THE TEXT

> › Believers find purpose and contentment by pursuing godliness.

> › Believers are to live in light of the promise of eternal life.

> › Believers are to use their resources to bless others.

Reflect on 1 Timothy 6:10. Ask God to show you any areas of your life in which your love is misguided. Memorize the verse.

As a group, identify needs in your community that your Bible-study group can address with your resources. What actions do you need to take to address those needs?

What changes can you make to honor Christ so that your earthly resources enhance Kingdom opportunities locally and globally?

❯ DAILY EXPLORATION

Day 1: Pursue contentment in Christ.

Read 1 Timothy 6:6-10, noting where true contentment lies.

Paul gave two reasons to pursue godliness.

1. "We brought nothing into the world, and we can take nothing out" (v. 7). None of the world's luxuries can be carried into eternity.

2. Godliness and contentment are nurtured through simplicity. Some people spend their lives trying to amass wealth and possessions.

Money itself is morally neutral. There's nothing wrong with money. Money can be used for good to secure shelter for those who are homeless, food for those who are starving, and medicine for those who are sick. Money can be used to build schools, seminaries, churches, and hospitals. It can support missionaries and church leaders as they spread the gospel and disciple believers.

However, money can also be used wrongly to violate justice, oppress the poor, abuse the innocent, corrupt the meek, slander the virtuous, and gratify the flesh. Paul said some people who craved money "have wandered away from the faith" (v. 10). He didn't mean they lost their salvation. Rather, they were like sheep who wandered away from the shepherd, seeking greener pastures. Instead of finding contentment, they ended up restless and wounded.

What does it mean to base your contentment on Christ?

Day 2: Seek holy virtues.

Read 1 Timothy 6:11, identifying what believers should pursue.

Paul addressed Timothy as a "man of God." That title was a common Old Testament description of someone whom God appointed to proclaim His truth. Paul used it to remind Timothy of the sacred responsibilities God had given him. Paul commanded Timothy to pursue holy virtues. The verb *pursue* is an imperative designating strong and immediate action. *Righteousness* and *godliness* have distinctive meanings. The former indicates right standing with God that produces right conduct, while the latter indicates right living for God that reflects His character. *Faith* and *love* are intersecting virtues that reflect trust in Christ and selfless love for Him and for others. *Endurance* and *gentleness* were crucial leadership qualities essential for Timothy's effectiveness in ministry. *Endurance* refers to the vital perseverance of someone who remains loyal to Christ despite tribulation. *Gentleness* refers to a disposition of courteousness and tenderness as Timothy fulfilled his responsibility as pastor.

What steps can you take to pursue the qualities Paul identified to counter greed?

Day 3: Live faithfully until Jesus returns.

Read 1 Timothy 6:12-14, considering Christ's example.

God had called Timothy to salvation and to ministry. Timothy publicly declared his faith in Christ when he was saved and baptized. Furthermore, he testified about Christ "in the presence of many witnesses" (v. 12) when he surrendered to serve Christ in ministry on his ordination.

Paul urged Timothy to fulfill his calling because he was accountable to God, "who gives life to all" (v. 13). Furthermore, Timothy was accountable to Jesus Christ. When Pilate asked Jesus if He was the King of the Jews, He courageously replied that He was (see Matt. 27:11). Timothy was to model his faithfulness after Jesus' faithfulness.

Paul also charged Timothy to keep this command "without fault or failure" (1 Tim. 6:14). This command could have referred to Timothy's specific responsibility as a "man of God" (v. 11), as well as his responsibility to proclaim and defend the essential truths of the gospel. Paul instructed Timothy to live faithfully "until the appearing of our Lord Jesus Christ" (v. 14). Anticipation of Christ's return would inspire Timothy to give his best and to live each day to the fullest, as if it could be his last.

What godly goals do you need to set as you consider the bigger picture of salvation and Jesus' return?

Day 4: God is worthy of worship.

Read 1 Timothy 6:15-16, highlighting God's attributes.

In view of Christ's return, Paul's writing erupted in majestic praise to God. He expressed several attributes of God's greatness that would motivate Timothy's service. Timothy's effectiveness in ministry rested in the assurance that the One who's all-powerful would impart the power needed to complete the task.

God is also "the King of kings, and the Lord of lords" (v. 15). This title was used to refer to God in the Old Testament (see Deut. 10:17; Ps. 136:2-3; Dan. 2:47) as well as to God the Son in the New Testament (see Rev. 17:14; 19:16). Kings rule over people and impose their will on them. God is the King who exerts His rule over all human kings.

God alone is immortal. Although God gives eternal life to believers, their physical lives began with His creation. Only God is without beginning or ending. This doxology reflects the adoration of God with which Paul began this letter (see 1 Tim. 1:17). Paul continually found himself overwhelmed by God's majesty. He closed his praise by ascribing to God "honor and eternal power" (6:16). God is worthy of our worship because He rules and reigns forever.

How does focusing on Jesus and His character help you fulfill God's purposes?

Day 5: Believers should be good stewards.

Read 1 Timothy 6:17-19, identifying what God wants believers to do with wealth.

Paul knew wise stewardship of all possessions is an eternal investment. Believers who invest in eternity store up for themselves a good foundation. Believers fail or succeed in their stewardship to the measure of their conviction that everything belongs to God. Consequently, a faithful steward in Ephesus understood what it means to take hold of "what is truly life" (v. 19). Followers of Christ who lived in the shadow of first-century wealth could testify that real life—abundant life (see John 10:10)—didn't reside in the fleeting pleasures of materialism but in a relationship with the Savior now and forever.

 KEY DOCTRINE: Stewardship >> God is the source of all blessings, temporal and spiritual; all we have and are, we owe to Him (see Deut. 8:18).

In what ways can you leverage your financial resources to spread the gospel and strengthen the church?

You have made us for Yourself, and our hearts are restless until they find their rest in You.

AUGUSTINE

❯ OBEY THE TEXT

Reflect on the truths found in 1 Timothy 6 and record your responses to the following questions or discuss them with two other members of your Bible-study group.

What barriers should we remove to achieve contentment? What bridges should we erect to reach it?

What does Paul's description of fleeing and fighting tell us about the goal of achieving true riches?

Although the Bible doesn't teach that wealth is inherently evil, how do Paul's warnings for the wealthy apply in everyday life?

MEMORIZE

The love of money is a root of all kinds of evil, and by craving it, some have wandered away from the faith and pierced themselves with many griefs.

1 TIMOTHY 6:10

MY THOUGHTS

Record insights and questions from this session's group experience
and daily exploration.

_____
_____
_____
_____
_____
_____
_____

MY RESPONSE

Note specific ways you'll put into practice the truth explored this week.

_____
_____
_____
_____
_____
_____
_____

MY PRAYERS

List specific prayer needs and answers to remember this week.

_____
_____
_____
_____
_____
_____
_____
_____

GETTING STARTED

OPENING OPTIONS: Choose one of the following to open the group discussion.

WEEKLY QUOTATION DISCUSSION STARTER: "The most important thought that ever occupied my mind is that of my individual responsibility to God."—Daniel Webster

> › Have you recently experienced this idea, even this past week? How have you experienced the truth expressed by this quotation?

> › What thoughts compete with God for your attention?

Life requires a constant process of evaluation and prioritization. Everything we do overflows from the thoughts and desires that occupy our hearts and minds. What we give our attention to determines what we choose to live for and whom we choose to become.

CREATIVE ACTIVITY: Before the session consider wise advice you've received over the years. Also consider advice you wish you'd been given. After the group arrives, share your examples. Then use the following questions and statements to get people involved and to focus on this week's concepts.

> › If you could go back in time and give yourself advice, what would it be?

> › What's the best advice anyone ever gave you? What made the wisdom especially meaningful or valuable?

As we begin the study, keep in mind the idea of trusted advice and proven wisdom. The first letter to Timothy was written from the apostle Paul's close personal relationship with the young leader and from a desire for him to succeed in a challenging context.

UNDERSTAND THE CONTEXT

PROVIDE BACKGROUND: Briefly introduce members to 1 Timothy, pointing out major themes, information, and ideas that will help them understand 1 Timothy 1:3-17 (see pp. 5 and 7). Then, to help people personally connect today's context with the original context, use the following questions.

> › How does understanding the relationship between Paul and Timothy help you discern Paul's tone of voice and intent in writing a letter full of instruction?

> › How does identifying the original context of this letter (and any book of the Bible) help us correctly understand and apply the text in our lives today?

❯ EXPLORE THE TEXT

READ THE BIBLE: Ask two volunteers to read 1 Timothy 1:3-17.

DISCUSS: Use the following questions to discuss group members' initial reactions to the text.

> What immediately stands out to you in this text as a theme or primary point?

> What words are used to describe improper teaching in verses 3-7? How does verse 5 describe the motives and goals of proper teaching? What strikes you most about the contrast between the two types of teaching and teachers?

> Why would Paul emphasize doctrine in the opening sentences to Timothy? What does that emphasis reveal about the nature of the church and the Christian life?

> What does Paul's statement in verses 13-16 reveal about salvation? Why was it important for Paul to establish these foundational truths in the opening sentences of his first letter to Timothy?

> What else does this text teach us about God? About ourselves?

> What do you find encouraging, timely, or convicting?

> What other questions or observations do you have?

NOTE: Provide ample time for group members to share responses and questions about the text. Don't feel pressured to prioritize the printed agenda over group members' personal experiences. If time allows, discuss responses to the questions in the personal reading.

❯ OBEY THE TEXT

RESPOND: Foster an environment of openness and action. Help individuals apply biblical truth to specific areas of personal thought, attitude, and/or behavior.

> What emotions and thoughts did you experience as you read Paul's declaration of unworthiness? In what ways have you been affected by other people's testimonies?

> Whom has God used to encourage and mentor you spiritually? Who in your life could use encouragement and spiritual guidance?

> What will you do to commit yourself to growing in godliness and truth during this study?

PRAY: Confess your unworthiness of God's grace and declare your overwhelming gratitude for His love. Praise God for saving you and making you a part of His kingdom. Ask for a passionate focus on the gospel of Jesus in your life, in your church, and in your interaction with the people around you.

› GETTING STARTED

OPENING OPTIONS: Choose one of the following to open the group discussion.

WEEKLY QUOTATION DISCUSSION STARTER: "True prayer is not a mere mental exercise, nor a vocal performance, but it is deeper far than that—it is spiritual commerce with the Creator of heaven and earth."—Charles H. Spurgeon

› Have you recently experienced this idea, even this past week? How have you experienced the truth expressed by this quotation?

› Why is it essential to remind ourselves of the nature of prayer in our daily lives?

If we're going to represent the character and truth of Jesus, we have to be in constant personal fellowship with Him. Communication is an essential part of any healthy relationship.

CREATIVE ACTIVITY: Before the session make a list of at least four popular brands, businesses, celebrities, or schools. After the group arrives, use the following questions and statements to get people involved and to focus on this week's concepts.

› What immediately comes to mind when you hear the word _____?

Repeat this question for each item on your list. Allow this activity to be as fun or as serious as the personality of your group allows.

› What might come to mind when someone hears your name? What would you want to come to someone's mind?

› What comes to mind when you hear the word *Jesus? Gospel? Church?* A reference to this group?

Today we'll consider the importance of the way we represent God in the world.

› UNDERSTAND THE CONTEXT

PROVIDE BACKGROUND: Briefly introduce members to major themes, information, and ideas that will help them understand 1 Timothy 2 (see p. 17). Then, to help people personally connect today's context with the original context, use the following question and statement.

› What natural problems may arise in a new community composed of different social classes, genders, professions, and backgrounds?

Paul instructed Timothy about the importance of order in the midst of new liberties and unity.

❯ EXPLORE THE TEXT

READ THE BIBLE: Ask a male volunteer to read 1 Timothy 2:1-8 and a female volunteer to read 1 Timothy 2:9-15.

DISCUSS: Use the following questions to discuss group members' initial reactions to the text.

> What immediately stands out to you in this text as a theme or primary point?

> What types of prayers are mentioned in verse 1? Why did Paul emphasize prayer before his instruction on behavior and character?

> What's meant by "tranquil and quiet" in verse 2? How do these words relate to a public Christian witness?

> What does the specific nature of Paul's instruction to both men and women suggest was happening in the Ephesian church and culture? What was he emphasizing?

> What else does this text teach us about God? About ourselves?

> What do you find encouraging, timely, or convicting?

> What other questions or observations do you have?

NOTE: Provide ample time for group members to share responses and questions about the text. Don't feel pressured to prioritize the printed agenda over group members' personal experiences. If time allows, discuss responses to the questions in the personal reading.

❯ OBEY THE TEXT

RESPOND: Foster an environment of openness and action. Help individuals apply biblical truth to specific areas of personal thought, attitude, and/or behavior.

> On a scale of 1 to 10, 1 being like culture and 10 being like Christ, how different would people say you look from the world? Why did you rate yourself this way?

> What have you found most helpful in developing a meaningful habit of prayer?

PRAY: Ask God to give you a humble heart and a hunger for time with Him. Specifically pray for your witness to the people around you and for the people whom group members identified last week as needing encouragement and spiritual guidance.

❯ GETTING STARTED

OPENING OPTIONS: Choose one of the following to open the group discussion.

WEEKLY QUOTATION DISCUSSION STARTER: "The way to gain a good reputation is to endeavor to be what you desire to appear."—Socrates

> › Have you recently experienced this idea, even this past week? How have you experienced the truth expressed by this quotation?

> › Why is a good reputation especially important for people in leadership? Do you think reputation in church leadership is more, less, or equally important as it is in roles of leadership in business, sports, and government?

This week we'll build on the ideas of personal character and public witness, specifically focusing on church leaders.

CREATIVE ACTIVITY: Before the session, consider the necessary qualifications for your most recent job. After the group arrives, share your example. Then use the following questions and statement to get people involved and to focus on this week's concepts.

> › What experiences and skills were necessary preparation for your most recent job?

> › If you're in charge of hiring employees to work with you, what qualities and skills would you consider most important?

Today we'll learn what the Bible says about essential qualifications for leaders of the local church.

❯ UNDERSTAND THE CONTEXT

PROVIDE BACKGROUND: Briefly introduce members to major themes, information, and ideas that will help them understand 1 Timothy 3:1-13 (see p. 27). Then, to help people personally connect today's context with the original context, use the following questions.

> › Why would Paul have felt the need to provide Timothy with a description of qualifications for church leaders?

> › If you had to choose a single trait for church leaders, what would it be? Why?

❯ EXPLORE THE TEXT

READ THE BIBLE: Ask two volunteers to read 1 Timothy 3:1-13.

DISCUSS: Use the following questions to discuss group members' initial reactions to the text.

> ❯ What immediately stands out to you in this text as a theme or primary point?

> ❯ How could Paul praise the desire to be a leader in verse 1 after teaching on humility in chapter 2?

> ❯ Identify each qualification Paul listed for overseers in verses 1–7. Why is each one important in the church and in the community? How is this list similar to or different from the qualifications for deacons in verses 8-13?

> ❯ Would you agree that most or all of the qualifications for leaders apply to expectations for any Christian? Are any of the qualifications unique to leaders? What does your answer reveal about Christian leadership?

> ❯ What else does this text teach us about God? About ourselves?

> ❯ What do you find encouraging, timely, or convicting?

> ❯ What other questions or observations do you have?

NOTE: Provide ample time for group members to share responses and questions about the text. Don't feel pressured to prioritize the printed agenda over group members' personal experiences. If time allows, discuss responses to the questions in the personal reading.

❯ OBEY THE TEXT

RESPOND: Foster an environment of openness and action. Help individuals apply biblical truth to specific areas of personal thought, attitude, and/or behavior.

> ❯ What leaders have been most influential in your life? What traits made them influential? What are you most grateful for among your church leaders?

> ❯ What needs exist in your church? How can you as individuals or as a group help meet those needs?

PRAY: Thank God for the blessing of your local church. Pray for faithfulness and integrity among the leaders and members of your church. Ask the Lord to raise up additional leaders, even among your own group, to advance gospel ministry.

❯ GETTING STARTED

OPENING OPTIONS: Choose one of the following to open the group discussion.

WEEKLY QUOTATION DISCUSSION STARTER: "Every day that we are not practicing godliness we are being conformed to the world of ungodliness around us."—Jerry Bridges

- ❯ Have you recently experienced this idea, even this past week? How have you experienced the truth expressed by this quotation?

- ❯ What does the word *practicing* clarify about godliness and ungodliness?

Today we'll learn what the Bible says about the importance of practicing godliness and the dangers of allowing worldliness to creep into our lives as individuals and as a church.

CREATIVE ACTIVITY: Before the session check your spam folder for a suspicious email subject or take a screenshot of a suspicious advertisement in your social-media feed, being careful not to click on anything suspicious. After the group arrives, share your example. Then use the following questions and statement to get people involved and to focus on this week's concepts.

- ❯ How do spammers and scammers try to get you to open an email or a web link?

- ❯ Have you ever fallen for a scam or false advertisement? If so, what was it? Why did you fall for it? Did you suspect it wasn't legitimate?

Today we'll learn what the Bible says about false teachers and their attempts to deceive Christians and churches.

❯ UNDERSTAND THE CONTEXT

PROVIDE BACKGROUND: Briefly introduce members to major themes, information, and ideas that will help them understand 1 Timothy 4:1-13 (see p. 37). Then, to help people personally connect today's context with the original context, use the following questions.

- ❯ Why would the early church be susceptible to false teaching?

- ❯ Why are we still susceptible to false teaching today? What are some examples in our culture of so-called Christian teachings that are false?

❯ EXPLORE THE TEXT

READ THE BIBLE: Ask two volunteers to read 1 Timothy 4:1-13.

DISCUSS: Use the following questions to discuss group members' initial reactions to the text.

- ❯ What immediately stands out to you in this text as a theme or primary point?

- > What makes teaching false in the deceptive sense of the word rather than merely mistaken? What did Paul identify as the origin of false teaching in verse 1? What did he say about the consciences of false teachers in verse 2?

- > Each person of the Trinity is mentioned in this text. What's the role of the Holy Spirit in the Christian life? Of God? Of Jesus? How is each one vital to a healthy Christian life?

- > What can we conclude from Paul's consistent emphasis on belief, personal behavior, and witness?

- > How do Paul's final instructions to Timothy in verses 11-13 emphasize the unique role of pastoral leadership described last week in chapter 3?

- > What else does this text teach us about God? About ourselves?

- > What do you find encouraging, timely, or convicting?

- > What other questions or observations do you have?

NOTE: Provide ample time for group members to share responses and questions about the text. Don't feel pressured to prioritize the printed agenda over group members' personal experiences. If time allows, discuss responses to the questions in the personal reading.

❯ OBEY THE TEXT

RESPOND: Foster an environment of openness and action. Help individuals apply biblical truth to specific areas of personal thought, attitude, and/or behavior.

- > What did Paul say are the benefit of and motivation for spiritual discipline and maturity? What happens if we're missing either the right discipline or the right motivation?

- > What areas of the spiritual life get the most attention when we pursue discipline and training in godliness? What areas tend to be the most neglected or hardest to practice? What habits have been especially helpful in your spiritual growth?

- > In which area do you need the most prayerful support from this group in order to set a better example for believers—speech, conduct, love, faith, or purity?

PRAY: Praise God for creating you and for revealing the truth in His Word. Pray for His Spirit to guide and empower you in godliness and discernment. Ask Him for joyful motivation and intentionality in spiritual discipline as you serve Jesus and set an example for others.

❯ GETTING STARTED

OPENING OPTIONS: Choose one of the following to open the group discussion.

WEEKLY QUOTATION DISCUSSION STARTER: "Giving is the secret to a healthy life. Not necessarily money, but whatever a person has to give of encouragement, sympathy, and understanding." —John D. Rockefeller Jr.

> ❯ Have you recently experienced this idea, even this past week? How have you experienced the truth expressed by this quotation?

> ❯ When have you been blessed by someone who had nothing tangible to offer?

Today we'll learn what the Bible says about caring for the needs of others, especially people who depend most on the church community.

CREATIVE ACTIVITY: Before the session reflect on your own answers to the following questions. After the group arrives, start by sharing your answers. Then use the following questions and statement to get people involved and to focus on this week's concepts.

> ❯ When you were younger, what did you most look forward to when you got older? Why was that prospect so appealing?

> ❯ Now that you're older, what do you miss most about being younger? Why is that memory so appealing? Why didn't you value that quality, experience, ability, or relationship more at the time?

Today we'll learn what the Bible says about relating to men and women who are older and younger than ourselves.

❯ UNDERSTAND THE CONTEXT

PROVIDE BACKGROUND: Briefly introduce members to major themes, information, and ideas that will help them understand 1 Timothy 5:1-8,17-21 (see p. 47). Then, to help people personally connect today's context with the original context, use the following questions and statements.

> ❯ Paul concluded chapter 4 by commanding Timothy, "Don't let anyone despise your youth, but set an example for the believers" (v. 12). Why would Paul immediately begin chapter 5 by instructing Timothy on relating to people older and younger than himself?

> ❯ Whom do you have a harder time paying attention to—people older or younger than you? Why do you find it easier to listen to or talk to the opposite age group? Why is it important to relate to both groups and not just our peers?

❯ EXPLORE THE TEXT

READ THE BIBLE: Ask two volunteers to read 1 Timothy 5:1-8,17-21.

DISCUSS: Use the following questions to discuss group members' initial reactions to the text.

> What immediately stands out to you in this text as a theme or primary point?

> What can you conclude from the fact that Paul addressed the needs of widows in verses 3-8 and elders in verses 17-21? What specific instructions did Paul give for relating to each group?

> How do Paul's instruction reflect Jesus' example? How are they consistent with God's instructions in the Old Testament?

> According to this text, how would you summarize the value of family? The value of church? The responsibility of all believers to actively support brothers and sister in Christ?

> What else does this text teach us about God? About ourselves?

> What do you find encouraging, timely, or convicting?

> What other questions or observations do you have?

NOTE: Provide ample time for group members to share responses and questions about the text. Don't feel pressured to prioritize the printed agenda over group members' personal experiences. If time allows, discuss responses to the questions in the personal reading.

❯ OBEY THE TEXT

RESPOND: Foster an environment of openness and action. Help individuals apply biblical truth to specific areas of personal thought, attitude, and/or behavior.

> What did you learn from this passage about how to handle conflict or sensitive issues with others? With which do you struggle most—attitude or action? What's one relationship you can be proactive in healing or improving through respectful care?

> How can we be intentional as a group to show love and respect to members who are older and to members who are younger?

PRAY: Thank God for His undeserved grace and abundant love toward you. Pray for a spiritual awareness of and a Christlike attitude toward the people around you. Ask for boldness, humility, and generosity in loving others as God loves you.

❯ GETTING STARTED

OPENING OPTIONS: Choose one of the following to open the group discussion.

WEEKLY QUOTATION DISCUSSION STARTER: "You have made us for Yourself, and our hearts are restless until they find their rest in You."—Augustine

> ❯ Have you recently experienced this idea, even this past week? How have you experienced the truth expressed by this quotation?

> ❯ At what point in your life have you been the most restless? How did God reveal Himself in a fresh, satisfying way, or how is He doing so now?

Today we'll learn what the Bible says about the difference between living for created things and living for the Creator.

CREATIVE ACTIVITY: Before the session recall how long you've had your cell phone. After the group arrives, use the following questions and statement to get people involved and to focus on this week's concepts.

> ❯ How long have you had your cell phone? What made you get a new one? Are you already wondering what the next one will be like?

> ❯ Do you think access to technology like our cell phones is positive, negative, or neutral in relation to our lives—spiritually, emotionally, and practically? Would you say technology has made you more, less, or equally content as you were before you had it?

The point isn't really about the value of technology but about our contentment. Today we'll examine contentment by considering the joy of an eternal perspective rather than a temporal one.

❯ UNDERSTAND THE CONTEXT

PROVIDE BACKGROUND: Briefly introduce members to major themes, information, and ideas that will help them understand 1 Timothy 6:6-19 (see p. 57). Then, to help people personally connect today's context with the original context, use the following questions and statements.

> ❯ After Paul instructed Timothy in chapter 5 about how the church should care for one another, especially widows and pastors, what would the natural fear or hesitation be for taking care of other people financially?

> ❯ In what ways does our culture promote the idea that we don't have enough money, possessions, or resources? Do you think our culture today is more, less, or equally concerned about material needs and comforts as Paul and Timothy's culture in Ephesus?

❯ EXPLORE THE TEXT

READ THE BIBLE: Ask two volunteers to read 1 Timothy 6:6-19.

DISCUSS: Use the following questions to discuss group members' initial reactions to the text.

> What immediately stands out to you in this text as a theme or primary point?

> How do these verses summarize the major themes Paul addressed throughout 1 Timothy?

> Why did Paul go into detail describing Jesus in verses 13-16? Which descriptions are most meaningful to you? Why?

> Why did Paul go into detail describing eternal life in verses 12-19? What descriptions are most meaningful to you? Why?

> What else does this text teach us about God? About ourselves?

> What do you find encouraging, timely, or convicting?

> What other questions or observations do you have?

NOTE: Provide ample time for group members to share responses and questions about the text. Don't feel pressured to prioritize the printed agenda over group members' personal experiences. If time allows, discuss responses to the questions in the personal reading.

❯ OBEY THE TEXT

RESPOND: Foster an environment of openness and action. Help individuals apply biblical truth to specific areas of personal thought, attitude, and/or behavior.

> How are you struggling with contentment? How have you experienced the joy and freedom of contentment in Christ? What competes most with Christ for your attention and affection?

> What has been your greatest takeaway from studying 1 Timothy? What has God revealed about Himself? About you? What have you put into practice as a result of this study?

> In keeping with Paul's ongoing reminder that our Christian lives are not only about ourselves but also about our example for, witness to, and influence on others, whom do you know who needs to hear and experience what you've learned and experienced by studying 1 Timothy? Will you commit to share with them personally? Whom can you invite to join us for our next study?

PRAY: Praise God for the incomparable joy and value of knowing Jesus now and the awesome hope of spending eternal life with Him in the future. Thank Him for generously providing all of your needs and for giving you the opportunity to join His work by blessing others physically and spiritually. As you commit to live wholeheartedly for the glory of Jesus, pray that everyone around you will recognize the clear difference between the church and the world.

TIPS FOR LEADING A GROUP

PRAYERFULLY PREPARE

Prepare for each session by—

> **reviewing the weekly material and group questions ahead of time;**

> **praying for each person in the group.**

Ask the Holy Spirit to work through you and the group discussion to help people take steps toward Jesus each week as directed by God's Word.

MINIMIZE DISTRACTIONS

Create a comfortable environment. If group members are uncomfortable, they'll be distracted and therefore not engaged in the group experience. Plan ahead by taking into consideration—

> **seating;**

> **temperature;**

> **lighting;**

> **food or drink;**

> **surrounding noise;**

> **general cleanliness (put pets away if meeting in a home).**

At best, thoughtfulness and hospitality show guests and group members they're welcome and valued in whatever environment you choose to gather. At worst, people may never notice your effort, but they're also not distracted. Do everything in your ability to help people focus on what's most important: connecting with God, with the Bible, and with others.

INCLUDE OTHERS

Your goal is to foster a community in which people are welcome just as they are but encouraged to grow spiritually. Always be aware of opportunities to—

> **invite** new people to join your group;

> **include** any people who visit the group.

An inexpensive way to make first-time guests feel welcome or to invite people to get involved is to give them their own copies of this Bible-study book.

ENCOURAGE DISCUSSION

A good small group has the following characteristics.

> **Everyone participates.** Encourage everyone to ask questions, share responses, or read aloud.

> **No one dominates—not even the leader.** Be sure what you say takes up less than half of your time together as a group. Politely redirect discussion if anyone dominates.

> **Nobody is rushed through questions.** Don't feel that a moment of silence is a bad thing. People often need time to think about their responses to questions they've just heard or to gain courage to share what God is stirring in their hearts.

> **Input is affirmed and followed up.** Make sure you point out something true or helpful in a response. Don't just move on. Build personal connections with follow-up questions, asking how other people have experienced similar things or how a truth has shaped their understanding of God and the Scripture you're studying. People are less likely to speak up if they fear that you don't actually want to hear their answers or that you're looking for only a certain answer.

> **God and His Word are central.** Opinions and experiences can be helpful, but God has given us the truth. Trust Scripture to be the authority and God's Spirit to work in people's lives. You can't change anyone, but God can. Continually point people to the Word and to active steps of faith.

KEEP CONNECTING

Think of ways to connect with members during the week. Participation during the session is always improved when members spend time connecting with one another away from the session. The more people are comfortable with and involved in one another's lives, the more they'll look forward to being together. When people move beyond being friendly and in the same group to truly being friends who form a community, they come to each session eager to engage instead of merely attending.

Encourage group members with thoughts, commitments, or questions from the session by connecting through—

> emails;

> texts;

> social media.

When possible, build deeper friendships by planning or spontaneously inviting group members to join you outside your regularly scheduled group time for—

> meals;

> fun activities;

> projects around your home, church, or community.

GROUP CONTACT INFORMATION

Name _____ Number _____
Email/social media _____

Name _____ Number _____
Email/social media _____

Name _____ Number _____
Email/social media _____

Name _____ Number _____
Email/social media _____

Name _____ Number _____
Email/social media _____

Name _____ Number _____
Email/social media _____

Name _____ Number _____
Email/social media _____

Name _____ Number _____
Email/social media _____

Name _____ Number _____
Email/social media _____

Name _____ Number _____
Email/social media _____

Name _____ Number _____
Email/social media _____